F.B.I.

(Favor, Blessing, Increase)

Living Abundantly By Unlocking
God's Favor In Your Life

BARBARA BRYANT

Unless otherwise noted, all Scriptures taken from the King James Version of the Bible.

Definitions are taken from Webster's American English Dictionary,
New Edition copyright 2011 by Federal Street Press

WestBow Press books may be ordered through booksellers or by contacting:

WestBow Press
A Division of Thomas Nelson
1663 Liberty Drive
Bloomington, IN 47403
www.westbowpress.com
1 (866) 928-1240

ISBN: 978-1-4908-1321-9 (sc)
ISBN: 978-1-4908-1323-3 (hc)
ISBN: 978-1-4908-1322-6 (e)

Library of Congress Control Number: 2013919025

Printed in the United States of America.

WestBow Press rev. date: 10/29/2013

Contents

$

Acknowledgments

My deepest appreciation goes to those who made it possible for me to write about my incredible experience of understanding God's favor, blessing, and increase. My thanks are extended—

To my sons, Steven and Stedmon, you continue to provide fresh lenses through which to view the world. What a joy it is to pray for you and watch the incredible things God does in your lives! You have made my life a joy beyond measure. I love you.

To my mother, Jessie Stewart, and in memory of my father, Charlie, you gave me a foundation in life that helped me become who I am today.

To the staff and board members of Barbara Bryant Ministries and the Gifted to Be a Gift Foundation, thank you for your unwavering support and faithfulness. It is such a peaceful pleasure to work with each of you.

I want to especially thank Pastor James A. Lewis and Mother Barbara McCoo Lewis. Thanks for your tremendous role model as spiritual leaders. You have taught me so much about ministry and have had such an influence in preparing me to know the heart and timing of God.

I am grateful to Bishop Joe L. Ealy, who agreed to contribute a foreword to this book. It is an incredible honor to have his words grace these pages.

Most importantly, to my Lord, the author and finisher of my faith, how can words adequately acknowledge all You have done for me and through me. I love You more than I am able to express. Without You, I can do nothing.

$

Foreword

by Bishop Joe L. Ealy

Our Lord personally chose twelve men and invested most of His energies in them. This is also true of Barbara Bryant. She is a chosen author purposed to express the love of God to this generation. Despite the obstacles, she triumphed and fulfilled her task.

FBI is the results of many people who have made an investment in her dream. This book reflects her creativity and a personal journey of her life.

FBI is a unique and valuable guide. You will discover the provision God has made just for you in every facet of life through His "exceeding great and precious promises" (2 Peter 1:4). Her message will have a powerful influence upon your life.

FBI pulls back the curtain for all of us to see behind the scenes. You will be both challenged and inspired by this book; it will be a tremendous blessing to all who will read it.

Enjoy these strong positive teachings on favor. The favor of God is not only available to the believer, it is a promise.

As her Jurisdictional Bishop, I have known her most of her adult life and couldn't be more proud of her.

Bishop Joe L. Ealy
Jurisdictional Prelate
Southern California First Jurisdiction
Church of God in Christ

$

Introduction

You are probably reading this book because you have recognized a need to experience God's favor, blessings, and increase in your life. The good news is we do not have to be transmuted to heaven to experience the increasing *favor* of God. We can experience God's favor on earth. It is available to each of us who are in Christ Jesus.

I believe that God plays favorites, that certain people experience His blessings more abundantly than others. Ephesians 1:3 says, "Blessed be the God and Father of our Lord Jesus Christ, who has blessed us with every spiritual blessing in the heavenly places in Christ." The *you* and the *us* in this Scripture refers to those who are in the body of Christ. We have been so spiritually blessed in Jesus Christ. It's like being incredibly thirsty and finding a spring that will never run dry. It's like being lonely and finding a friend who will never leave you or forsake you. It's like needing to be accepted and finding one who knows you better than you know yourself and yet loves you and accepts you wholly and completely. It's like needing some guidance and finding the Good Shepherd. It's like needing some comfort and finding the Prince of Peace. God is partial to us because we are His children. He has blessed us in such a marvelous way.

The Bible says in Psalm 5:12, "For You, O Lord will bless the righteous; with favor You will surround him as with a shield." God has surrounded us with His favor. In a season during which resources and money seem to be in short supply, God has granted us with favor.

It is important to remember that our source is not this worlds system but God's abundant and endless resources, which He has made available to us as His heirs and His children. No matter what we hear about the world in which we live, we must always look at the current economy and situation through the eyes of God. When we do, we will see an abundant supply of more than enough for our every need or desire. We will also recognize that in God's economy, what appears to be lack, God has an endless supply. That endless supply is granted to His children.

According to Psalm 5:12, there is a favor shield. The Lord says His favor on His people is like a shield wrapped around them; however, it is for a particular group that are identified as the righteous. A *shield* is a protective structure or device—an outer covering. A shield was used by soldiers in times of battle. One did not walk around with a shield in peacetime. It was in battle that the shield was used as a defensive piece of armor, crucial for the soldier's survival. The shield was held up against the body to protect oneself from the enemy's offensive weapons.

The Christian life is not a walk through the daisies. We have a real enemy; therefore, we need a shield for protection. This shield of favor will not just protect us from the front but also the rear. It is a shield that surrounds us. Even when we don't know the Enemy's plan or scheme, God's divine favor will insulate us from damage and destruction. So ask yourself this question: "If the living God, Creator of everything, has supernaturally surrounded me with His favor and provision, why am I worried about the economy?" You have a God who can and will supply (fill to the full) your every need according to His riches in glory by Christ Jesus. This is not "name it and claim it" or "blab it and grab it." This is the promise of our heavenly Father to the believer.

As you read this book, I pray that the content will help turn favor, blessing, and increase into a manifestation of reality in your life. I pray that you will focus on preparing yourself for the manifestation of the promise. Why? This is your year of promise fulfillment. So *expect.* Yes, *expect.* Webster's American English Dictionary defines expectation as "a strong belief that something will happen in the future." It also means "to hope for what should happen." As you read this book, you should expend the following:

- Expect God to move with mighty wonders as He promised He would.
- Expect God to put you in the right place at the right time to meet the right person.
- Expect God to unlock your destiny.

- Expect God to take you from ordinary to extraordinary.
- Expect the goodness of the Lord at any time in your life.
- Expect God to pour his blessings out over you like a gigantic flood.
- Expect God to double your harvest, double your reward, and double your blessing.
- Expect favor and increase in your life
- Expect to be blessed . . . and blessed abundantly.

Don't defer your ability to prosper because your expectations have been wounded. Let go of limited thinking and come to expect God's best because that is what He wants for you. Are you ready for it? I pray that you are. Get ready to be blessed by *FBI.*

$

Prologue

Are you and I important to God? Does He really care, and if so, why? Men have asked such questions from the beginning of time. I believe that the answers to these important questions will change us forever. Join me, as together we examine the Holy Scripture to discover exactly how God feels about us and why.

In Psalm 115:12-14 we read, "The LORD hath been mindful of us; he will bless us; he will bless the house of Israel; he will bless the house of Aaron. He will bless them that fear the LORD, both small and great. The LORD shall increase you more and more, you and your children." This is the promise of God to those who love Him and are called according to His purposes—you and me.

$

Chapter 1

In the Beginning

Can you imagine a time when nothing existed? Nothing! No universe, no atmosphere, no planets, no stars, sun, or moon. No earth, no light, and no water. In the beginning no one and nothing existed except God. He existed alone. It's a stunning thought, isn't it?

Genesis 1: 1 says, "In the beginning God—" At that time there was no heaven, where He is now manifest in all His glory. There was no earth to engage His attention. There were no angels to worship and proclaim His glory. There was no universe to be upheld by the word of His power. There was absolutely nothing—no one but God.

In the beginning marks the inception of time. *In the beginning* suggests that there existed a time before time that always was—and so too, God. *In the beginning* marks the event when God decided to create.

God marks the beginning. He came before the beginning, and He caused the beginning. The Bible begins with God. When everything else began, God was already there. He was the unbegun one, the unoriginated one. In the beginning God was there first.

God is always previous. We cannot think rightly of God until we begin to think of Him as always being *there* and being *there* first. Begin where we will, God is *there* first. He is Alpha and Omega, the beginning and the ending, which was and which is and which is to come. In one unified present glance He comprehends all things from everlasting, and He can see past, present, and future without moving His eyes. Very simply put, God sees and knows 100 percent of everything that can be seen and known because He was *there* first.

God has perfect knowledge of everything. He knows all things, for He is omniscient. He is everywhere, so He is omnipresent. Not only does God know all things, but He is before all things. And in Him all things are held together. One interpretation of Colossians 1:17 is that all is of God because God is always previous. The word *before* in the Scripture means "ahead of, earlier than, and previous to." When you expand the definition of the word *previous*, it means "earlier, prior, before, preceding, and already arranged." The Lord always goes out before you to ensure His plan for your life is prearranged, predetermined, and preplanned so that it will lead to a triumphal procession. Bottom line is that God is *there* before you and His previous workings always meet your present response.

- He is there before you get there.
- He knows before you know.
- He sees before you see it.
- He does before you do.
- He moves before you move.
- He healed before you became sick.
- He sent food before you got hungry.
- He provides before you need.
- He answered before you called.
- He knew you before you were formed.

What does all of this mean? God is preceding you. He is earlier than you. He is prior to you. He is before you, and He goes before you. God is always previous to ensure everything in your life is done according to His plan. He is always previous, so He can arrange and plan everything you will need in order to accomplish His plan in His kingdom.

When you truly understand that God is before you, you will take confidence in knowing that He will be for you. In the beginning God—

This is why God is different from every other kind of being. He never began. We can compare Him to nothing at all. He is *sui generis*, meaning "unique or in a class of its own." And in the beginning He gave to everything else form and substance, structure and life.

So during eternity past God was entirely alone. He was self-sufficient, completely self-satisfied, in need of nothing and no one else. I'm sure you want to ask this: "If God was alone, who made God?" Nothing at all created God. The living God is without beginning or end of days. He is from eternity to eternity. God Himself had no cause. He has no birthday, and He has no external life-support system. He is absolutely self-sufficient. He is the eternal, self-existent one. Before everything else there was God alone.

When God finally began His act of creation, it was obvious that He was the one creating. He didn't do it out of need. In fact, when He called it all into existence, it was only because, as a self-sufficient God, He desired it to be so. God alone *created* out of nothing. Somebody has said, "Out of nothing comes nothing." But out of God came the creation. The creation added nothing to God. Malachi 3:6 confirms this when it says, "For I am the Lord, I change not." God's glory could not be augmented, amplified, or diminished by anything He created.

I believe it's important to grasp the truth that when God was alone, He was under no constraint. He was under no obligation and no necessity to create anything or anyone. There was nothing and nobody else making any suggestions to Him, let alone helping Him. There was God alone, purposing and designing His creation.

That He chose to *create* was purely a sovereign act on His part—initiated by nothing outside of Himself and His own personal desires. It was determined only by His own good pleasure. The Bible says in Ephesians 1:11, "For He worketh all things after the counsel of His will." So everything God created was simply done to manifest His glory.

In Romans 11:34 Paul brings to a close a very long and complex argument on salvation by grace, ending it with this question: "Who hath known the mind of the Lord? Or who hath been His counselor?" The answer is an emphatic "No one." That's why men have been perpetually perplexed. They simply have never been able to figure God out because He operates on another level and in another dimension. As a result it is impossible to bring almighty God down to our level or describe Him accurately in mere words. And it is impossible to put God under any obligation to the creatures because God has absolutely nothing to gain from us.

In Job 35:7 the writer says this: "If you are righteous, what can you give God, or what can God get from your hand?" Your wickedness only affects humans like yourself and your righteousness only other people. They can add nothing to the essential glory of God because He is and has always been completely blessed in and of Himself.

Before we were ever born or called into being, God was complete. He is an absolutely complete being. *Absolute* means "no separation." Everything that exists is not separate from God. The Bible says in Colossians 1:17 that God is before all things and in Him all things hold together. He also upholds all things by the word of His power. In fact, all things were made by God, and without Him nothing was created except through Him.

We do not make God what He is by thinking a certain way about Him. We don't make Him. He makes us. We don't decide what He is going to be like. He decides what we are going to be like. He created the universe, and it has the meaning He gives it, not the meaning we give it.

God, who is omnipotent, needs nothing outside Himself in order to function. He needs absolutely nothing from His creation in order to operate. Again God has always been completely blessed in and of Himself. He is perfect providence and cosmic confidence. He is solitary in His majesty, unique in His excellence, and peerless in His perfection.

God maintains and sustains the balance of the universe. He knows no boundaries and no limits. He is without measure. He sustains all but is independent of all. He gives to all, but He is enriched by none. God is blessed in Himself, for He is all-knowing and all-powerful. Transcendence is who He is, for He is outside of space, matter, and time. We know Him as three in one—for He is Father, Son, and Holy Ghost. And His preeminence makes Him eternal and unable to be changed by forces within the universe

He is so far beyond the power of the human mind in understanding. We can't even imagine His greatness.

He is immutable, impartial, and incomprehensible.

He is far beyond our conception, thoughts, and language. He can be *known*, but He cannot be fully comprehended.

He is so independent that He doesn't *need* any of us.

Acts 17:25 emphatically declares that God "is not served by human hands, as if he needed anything." And yet before creation He consulted the Son and the Holy Spirit, and together they agreed on a plan. "Let us make man in our image" for the purpose of fellowship. That's how much they wanted our company.

It was King David, who wrote in Psalm 8, "When I look at your heavens, the work of your fingers, the moon and the stars, which you have set in place, What is man that you are mindful of him, and the son of man that you care for him? Yet you have made him a little lower than the heavenly beings and crowned him with glory and honor." In other words, "Who are we, and how is it that God consider us worthy of notice?"

Here David made it clear that God made us lower than only one created being—angels. In other words, we are from God's point of view the most valuable beings God ever created.

This begs the following questions:

1. What is it that makes man so valuable to God, the Creator of heaven and earth?
2. What is it about man that God would constantly keep him on His mind?
3. What is it about man that God makes so much of him?
4. What is it about man that God would pay him so much attention and vow never to leave him, visiting with him daily?

To be honest it seems inconceivable to me that an incomparable, omnipotent God who made both heaven and the earth should even be concerned with man. It blows my mind to realize that the Master of the universe would notice man, let alone consider him significant when man is little more than a fleeting microscopic dot on the planet.

"What is man, that Thou art mindful of him?" (Psalm 8:4)

$

Chapter 2

Who is Man?

Who is man that God would exalt him? What is a man to such an astounding God? Who is man that God would delight in him and want to spend intimate time in his company? What can possibly interest God in man? Why would God set His affections on and give His attentions to such vulnerable beings?

Who is man? What makes him valuable to God? Why is man constantly on God's mind? Why would God create man and vow to never leave him or forsake him? What is it about man that God would come down from heaven and fight on his behalf?

What are we that God should be mindful of us? After all, man is merely flesh that will perish and go the way of the grass of the field. Man is weak, frail, mortal, and incredibly unpredictable. God Himself said that no one should put confidence in man because he will inevitably fail every time.

As far as the angels are concerned, man is a most complex and confusing being. Ever since the fall he has been susceptible to sickness, death, bondage, and remarkably evil intentions—a manipulator and certainly arrogant and prideful in his attitudes. From the time he sinned, man was suddenly subject to the whims and deceptions of Satan. And because man has the ability to think, reason, and make decisions, he is also the center of a massive tug-of-war, between the two opposing forces of good and evil.

Whether we like to admit it or not, here are some indisputable facts about man:

- Give him time, and he will turn on you.
- Give him an inch, and he will make a fool of himself.
- He can go from anger to an act of goodness in a minute.
- He can travel from saneness to craziness in a moment.
- He can shift from energetic inspiration to pathetic depression in a second.
- He can do amazingly good deeds one minute and kill someone the next.
- He can go from passionate inspiration to the depths of despair in a split second.
- He can morph from sanity to lunacy at the drop of a hat.
- I'm a witness. Man can shout the highest praise to God in church and then cuss you out in the parking lot within the space of an hour.

It's no wonder then that man, the only creature God created by the words of His mouth, often seeks therapy and must repent! Animals never have to repent, for they have no consciousness of sin. The sun, the moon, or the stars don't require psychotherapy either. But God had to know ahead of time that man would often flip out with no forewarning whatsoever. Even knowing that, however, the Creator, the Master of the universe went on to create man and to take note of man, and to this day, He is continually mindful of him.

Man must be something. There must be some great and sufficient reason as to why the Maker of the universe should take so much interest in man. Evidently *bigness* is not *greatness*, and a tiny baby is worth more than the tallest mountain.

Man must have a value to God. He must occupy some role in God's divine plan. One might imagine that God would consider us less than worthless since we are sinners by nature. But that's not so! We are so valuable to God that He had placed His creation under the supervision of man. David wrote in Psalm 8:6, "You have made him (man) to have dominion over the works of Your hands; You have put all *things* under his feet." What is dominion? The Hebrew meaning denotes royalty, reign, rule, governing, as well as management. It implies that *things* submit to you. It also denotes having civil rule or ruling power and authority.

To get a deeper sense of that awe, think about how God values us despite our wayward ways. David said, "Thou crownedst him . . . . Thou madest him to have dominion . . . Thou hast put all things under his feet" (Psalm 8:5-6). It is clear that God has given us royal supremacy.

We are valued by God because we are His creation, made in His image and likeness (see Genesis 1). We have divine likeness. Having the *image* or *likeness* of God means in the simplest terms that we resemble God. God's image upon man consists of His nature. The Psalmist (8:5) spoke of man as being created a little lower than the angels. According to Genesis 1:27 man is created in the image of God; he is a being in the image of God. Since he is only a little less than divine, he is also only a little less than angelic. The psalmist's point was that man, because he bears the image of God, is indeed "patterned after Him."

Man, in fact, is the crowning achievement of God's creation. He is not insignificant to God. He was created for God's glory, and he is the object of God's love. Let's take a moment to examine all three facts.

Man Is Not Insignificant to God

Man is not insignificant to God. We were created uniquely, deliberately, and purposefully by Him. We're no accident or happenstance! So don't ever let the Enemy make you think that God does not want you. Don't ever doubt God's personal care for you. God ordered you into existence.

You may be feeling insignificant today, but I am writing to remind you that you are a top priority in God's mind. Your name may not be on a Hollywood billboard, but that does not mean you are not on God's VIP list.

I'll tell you as a living witness that God has not forgotten, forsaken, or abandoned you. People may have let you down through the years, but if you check God's track record, it will confirm that He has been faithful. Think about it. He remembered you in your lowest state. He was there in your darkest hours. He was there in your weakness moment. God came through in the end. He was right there when you felt helpless and hopeless. He was there when you felt desperate and dysfunctional. When all else failed, God was right there.

God held you together when your life was falling apart. He helped you stand up again when circumstances tried to knock you down. He even used the problem that tried to bring you down to build you back up again. You survive it all because God was there.

Not only was God there, but He was also thinking about you. Even though you might think otherwise, God is thinking about you, and He cares about what happens to you. The next time you wonder what the Lord really thinks about you, remember the time when He promoted you and others disqualified you. Recall the time when God brought you through trials and troubles, foreclosure and failure, recession and ruin. Rehearse in your mind the time when He brought you through conflicts and crises and healed you from sickness and disease.

I invite you to remember what the Lord has done for you. No matter how successful you may be, it was not your intelligence, charisma, networking, ministry position, career, or business that helped you become successful. It was nobody but God that did it. You wouldn't be who you are, you wouldn't have what you have, you couldn't do what you do, and you wouldn't know what you know if God had not been mindful (thinking) of you.

God is never disconnected from what's going on and what's going down in your life. He is not sitting somewhere distance and aloof on the throne in heaven with no interest or connection to what's happening with you.

What I want to make clear is the fact that God is active, engaged, and immersed in the affairs of humanity. There is not one thing that you have gone through that God has not taken notice of. God has noticed everything you have gone through and everything you will go through. Nothing you have experienced in your life has been outside of His attention. No problem, no issue, no pain, no sickness has escaped His notice. God sees you. He sees you up close and personal. He sees your public and private life. We cannot hide ourselves anywhere where God will not see us.

What does God see? He sees your hurt, your pain, your tears, and your sleepless nights. He has seen the times when you didn't know what to do or which way to turn. He has noticed the mistreatment of others toward you. He heard every lie the Enemy said about you. He saw every time the Enemy had you surrounded. God even saw the times you were backed up in a corner, feeling like you had no way out. But don't worry. God witnessed every injustice, and He wrote it all down in His mind. And when your hour has come, God will respond.

Man Was Created In The Image Of God to Reflect His Glory

Man was created in the image of God to reflect His glory. Isaiah 43:7 says, "I have created him for my glory, I have formed him; yea, I have made him." What then does it mean to say that God created us *for His glory*? It means that when God says He made us for His glory, He does not mean He made us so that He could become more glorious in Himself. Instead Isaiah 43:7 means is that He created us to display His glory—that is, so His glory might be known and praised.

Are you catching the vision, seeing the potential deep within you to walk in the power and glory? You may not be able to see it by looking in the mirror, but it's there. I guarantee it. When you accepted Christ as Savior, He gave you a gift and sent the Holy Spirit to live inside you. That's right. The manifest glory of God Himself lives in you!

Do you grasp what that means? It means that the very God of the universe Himself not only saved you from the clutches of sin, hell, and the grave but left part of Himself in the person of the Holy Spirit to cohabit your spirit so that you and He are one. It also means that everything God gave Jesus, He has given to you. In the same way everything in God's Word applies to you, and the Holy Spirit is your teacher, who, as you read and meditate on the Word, will explain, clarify, and give you revelation and understanding of exactly what it means to be "in Him."

Man Is The Object of God's Love

Man is also the object of God's love. This was the thing David was puzzling over. How can such a great and mighty God care about something as lowly as a man? The answer is love.

Real love—agape love has little to do with hearts and flowers, little to do with romance or heart-shaped boxes filled with chocolates as much as we might wish it were so—real love is something else altogether.

First John 4:8 says that God *is* love. *Love* is the one word that fully encompasses God's nature. Both the Old and New Testaments reaffirm repeatedly that He is completely filled with compassion. Psalm 86:15 confirms that He is a God full of compassion and graciousness, long-suffering and plenteous in mercy and truth.

To demonstrate that point, all we have to do is look at countless Old Testament stories of the children of Israel, who repeatedly went their own way, refusing God's plan for their lives. And yet He never responded to them in wrath but sought to restore them at every opportunity. And He's still doing the same thing today.

The word *compassion* means to have so much mercy and tenderness for others that it actually causes pain to see them suffer. Everything God does is motivated by that kind of deep compassion and love. From the beginning it was God's plan to create man, through whom He would perpetuate the love of God from generation to generation so that His glory would shine through and all men would be saved. And because He never changes, this plan is still in effect.

God does not love us for what He can get out of us. God has no needs. He simply loves us by an act of His will, which is the way we should love Him. Man is the creation of God's love, and because of that love, God is mindful of him.

$

Chapter 3

God is Mindful of Man

God has a lot on His plate, and yet He is mindful of you. The word *mindful* in Psalm 8:4 derives from the Hebrew word *zakar*, meaning "to think on, to hold in remembrance, to recognize, to set the heart upon, to keep continually in merciful view." How comforting then is it to know despite all the creations God watches over, He has you in His thoughts!

God's mind is full of you. He is preoccupied by you. His mind is always reflecting on the quality of His relationship with you and on all those things He can do to deepen, strengthen, enlarge, and enrich His relationship with you. We talk a lot about what we think of God, but have you ever asked yourself the question, "What does God think of me?" Maybe I should phrase it like this: "How does God think of me?" You may be wondering right now if God thinks about you at all.

In everything you do, God is thinking about you. You are in God's thoughts. According to the Psalm, He knows when you sit down and when you get up. He knows your thoughts before you think of them. In other words, before you say a word, God already knows what you are going to say. He knows what you are secretly thinking. He knows every movement you will make throughout the day. God knows everything you will do.

Psalm 139:17-18, reads, "How precious also are thy thoughts unto me, O God! how great is the sum of them! If I should count them, they are more in number than the sand: when I awake, I am still with thee." Have you ever tried to count the grains of sand on the seashore? It is absolutely impossible! There are so many in just a scoop of your hand that it becomes incomprehensible to think that we could even begin to count them. In this

Scripture verse the psalmist tells us that God's thoughts toward us even outnumber the grains of sand on the seashore! What imagery. The Father, who created you and who numbered all your days, is thinking about you all the time. He never stops thinking about you. And His thoughts are of love and adoration. How precious are His thoughts toward us!

God is the only one who can declare, "For I know the thoughts that I think toward you." And His thoughts toward us are greater, higher, and more glorious than we can ever comprehend. He said through Isaiah 55:8, "For My thoughts are not your thoughts, neither are your ways like My ways, says the Lord. For as the heavens are higher than the earth so are My ways higher than your ways and My thoughts higher than your thoughts." God's thoughts toward us are glorious, exalted, and wonderful.

Psalm 115:12 says, "The Lord hath been mindful of us." It is clear in this verse that God is aware of His children in the same way that a loving human father dotes on his children. He does so not because of anything we can do to be worthy but because He loves us for His own name's sake. One of our greatest needs as human beings is to be loved. We need to know that we are important to somebody, that somebody truly cares about us, wants us, and accepts us unconditionally. That somebody is God. God love us for His own namesake, and His love is the most powerful motivating force in all of His being.

God is complete and sufficient in and of Himself. He has no needs that must be met by others outside Himself. Therefore, He did not need to create other beings in order to express His love. But yet He created man, so He could communicate Himself to him, give of Himself for him, and bestow His very best on him for his benefit and blessing.

Psalm 139 (NIV) goes into great detail to show us exactly how He sees us.

> O Lord, you have searched me and you know me.
> You know when I sit and when I rise; you perceive my thoughts
> from afar.
> You discern my going out and my lying down; you are familiar
> with all my ways.
> Before a word is on my tongue you know it completely, O Lord.
> You hem me in—behind and before;
> You have laid your hand upon me.

Such knowledge is too wonderful for me, too lofty for me to attain.
Where can I go from your Spirit?
Where can I flee from your presence?
If I go up to the heavens, you are there; if I make my bed in the depths, you are there.
If I rise on the wings of the dawn, if I settle on the far side of the sea, even there your hand will guide me, your right hand will hold me fast.
If I say, "Surely the darkness will hide me and the light become night around me,"
Even the darkness will not be dark to you; the night will shine like the day, for darkness is as light to you.
For you created my inmost being; you knit me together in my mother's womb.
I praise you because I am fearfully and wonderfully made; your works are wonderful, I know that full well.
My frame was not hidden from you when I was made in the secret place.
When I was woven together in the depths of the earth, your eyes saw my unformed body.
All the days ordained for me were written in your book before one of them came to be.
How precious to me are your thoughts, O God!
How vast is the sum of them!
Were I to count them they would outnumber the grains of sand.
When I awake, I am still with you.

It should be of tremendous comfort to know you are always on God's mind. He is mindful of everything you're going through. He is ever alert to your needs and aware of your plight. In fact, you are so important to God that *He knows the very number of hairs on your head and the number of tracks in your weave.* More importantly God sees how amazing you truly are. He sees how much value, potential, and worth that is inside of you. This why you are constantly on His mind. Psalm 139:17 says, "You are thinking about me constantly." Hallelujah!

A. W. Tozer so aplty said, "An infinite God can give all of Himself to each of His children. He does not distribute Himself that each may have a part, but to each one He gives all of Himself as full as if there were no others."

God loves you so much that He gives all of Himself to you as if He has no other children. God likes you. He approves of you. He is thinking about your daily life and your future. How grateful we are to know that God is always thinking about us. God was thinking of us long before we ever thought of Him. And even today in times of confusion, pressure, or disappointment, He is thinking of us when we lose the handle on His presence, His love, and His watchful care over each one of us. We are always on His mind.

In case you're wondering, here is what God thinks:

- God thinks we are wonderfully made and marvelous in His sight (Psalm 139:14).
- God thinks so much of us that He adopted us into His family (Romans 8:15).
- We are the apple of God's eye (Zechariah 2:8).
- God thinks so much of us that He vowed to never leave us or forsake us (Hebrews 13:5).
- You are His child (John 1:12).

It is human nature to wonder what people think about you. But you should never have to wonder what God thinks about you.

Answer this question: How do you think God sees you? If you struggle to believe God loves you, it may be because you envision Him shaking His fist at you when you don't measure up. Perhaps that's the way you grew up, feeling inadequate, always wishing it were otherwise. Perhaps that's what your parents or other authority figures told you, but that's not how God sees you. He says He sees you through heaven's eyes, redeemed and made righteous by the blood of Jesus the moment you accepted His gift of salvation. He sees you with unlimited potential and has plans for you that are far greater than your wildest dreams.

If you feel inadequate as if God is down on you, you need to change the picture in your head and envision this instead: You're sitting, relaxing in a lawn chair alone in a peaceful meadow when Jesus walks toward you and smiles. He comes to where you're sitting, rests His hand gently on your head, and begins to sing a beautiful song of rejoicing over the day you were born, thanking God for you. If that picture doesn't strike a chord deep inside you, I don't know what will. Can you see it?

Whether or not you believe this scenario, it's true, so meditate on that and remind yourself that you are deeply loved more than you can even imagine. Tuck that truth deep in your spirit and bring it out any time the Devil accuses you or you feel tempted to accuse yourself or to wallow in perceived inadequacies or past failures. Those are merely lies of the Devil that can no longer victimize you unless you let them. In fact, the Devil was stripped of his dominion at the resurrection, so he can do absolutely nothing to you without your permission. So when he comes at you, tell him that enough is enough, that from this moment on you are going to walk according to the truth of God's Word and refuse to believe anything that doesn't agree with it.

God sees us through the filter of the blood of Jesus so that we can be confident of our status as heirs of the promise. That means you and I can go boldly to the throne, knowing we will be received, because as we learned earlier God has not only forgiven but also forgotten our past sinful, inadequate status, and welcomes us into His arms in the same way He welcomes Jesus—as if we had never sinned at all. God is mindful of us.

$

Chapter 4

Who are You?

Let me ask you this question: Who are you? There's no easy answer, is there? Before we go any further, I need to put to rest some common misconceptions in that regard. No matter what you believe, you are not worthless, an accident of fate, or the great-grandchild of a monkey. Such notions are unworthy of someone designed by the Master of the universe, so dump them right now. You are a one-of-a-kind, amazing individual for whom God also designed a destiny unlike anyone else's.

God could have made things much easier for Himself had He just used a cookie cutter and cut every human being out with exactly the same character, personalities, and responses much like the tin soldiers in *The Nutcracker Suite*. We certainly would have been more predictable and well-behaved if He had. But He didn't do that. From the very beginning He designed us to be distinct individuals with entirely different fingerprints and DNA sequences, as varied as we are numerous. Your DNA sequence is unique amongst all DNA sequences of any human who has ever lived and will live. That's because He absolutely delights in variety and creativity.

But you are unique. You are special. There is no one like you . . . ever. In a world of more than seven billion people, it might be difficult to believe that, but it's true. God created you as an individual. You may have been unplanned, but you are not an accident. You may even have had an illegitimate birth, but there is nothing random about you. No human being is a chance happening.

In His boundless creativity God does not have to repeat Himself because he has run out of ideas or resources. He didn't get to the three billionth person and get stuck creating someone different from all who were created before. Neither does He find Himself wondering what He's going to do with that three billionth child of His. No, He knows exactly how special you are in every way and what a special place you have in His heart long before you were conceived in your mother's womb. You are as special as any child of God, past, present, or future.

When speaking about our particular unique function in the body of Christ, Peter says that the grace of God is upon each one of us in a different way. He puts it this way: "As each one has received a gift, minister it to one another as good stewards of the manifold grace of God" (1 Peter 4:10). That word *manifold* means many-sided or multifaceted.

We have not been mass-produced. Each of us is individually handcrafted by God. And we were created with a purpose in mind.

You are a part of God's plan. God worked out his plan while Joseph was in prison, while Moses lay as a baby in a basket in the Nile, through an immoral, blinded Samson, through a shepherd's slingshot, through a divided kingdom, through a Jewess exile, through baby Jesus, whom a king wanted to kill, and He is working out His plan in your life as well.

What a difference it would make in the lives of men and women today if they knew that they were created and born with a special purpose and that God has a specific and unique plan for their lives. This knowledge literally set me free and gave me hope for my life. Looking back, I see how God used my painful experiences to birth purpose in my life. It was also through my trouble times that I discovered who I was in Christ.

You are important in the grand scheme of things. You are somebody special in the body of Christ. You have a special place on the earth, in heaven, and in God's heart.

- You are His child (John 1:12).
- You are a fellow heir with Christ (Romans 8:17).
- You are a new creature in Christ (2 Corinthians 5:17).
- You are chosen, holy, and blameless before God (Ephesians 1:4)
- You are God's workmanship created to produce good works (Ephesians 2:10).
- You are a partaker of His promise (Ephesians 5:30).
- You are a citizen of heaven (Philippians 3:20).

- You are complete in Christ (Colossians 2:10).
- You are chosen (Ephesians 1:4).
- You are a royal priesthood (1 Peter 2:9).
- You are more than a conqueror (Romans 8:37).
- You are blessed with every spiritual blessing in the heavenly realms (Ephesians 1:3).

You are the select of God by His grace. You have been purchased with the highest price ever and then given everything in the kingdom of God. That's how important you are to God's vision. Amazing!

$

Chapter 5

The Glory of God in You

Are you catching the vision, seeing the potential deep within you to walk in the power and glory? You may not be able to see it by looking in the mirror, but it's there. I guarantee it. When you accepted Christ as Savior, He gave you a gift and sent the Holy Spirit to live inside you. That's right—the manifest glory of God Himself lives in you!

Paul describes in Ephesians 5:27, "a glorious church, not having spot, or wrinkle, or any such thing; but . . . holy and without blemish." Praise God! As born-again believers, we have the hope of glory! That means we can confidently expect the fullness of God's manifest presence in our lives. We don't have to just wish for it or read about other people who have experienced it. We can live in God's glory ourselves. We can do this because Jesus, the Anointed One, the Lord of glory Himself, lives inside every one of us.

The God of the universe not only saved you from the clutches of sin, hell, and the grave but that He left part of Himself in the person of the Holy Spirit to cohabit your spirit so that you and He are one. It also means that everything God gave Jesus, He has given to you. In the same way, everything in God's Word applies to you, and the Holy Spirit is your teacher, who, as you read and meditate on the Word of God, will explain, clarify, and give you revelation and understanding of exactly what it means to be "in Him."

This should give new meaning to the words, "I will never leave or forsake you," knowing He meant it in the most profound way ever. If we give it a meaning different from His, we are fools.

Throughout the Holy Scripture you discover that "I will never leave you nor forsake you" is one of the most frequent promises in the Bible. Quite often God says in His Word, "I will be with you." Before Adam and Eve ever sinned, they were promised God's presence. This promise was also made to Enoch who "walked with God." It was made to Noah, Abraham and Sarah, Jacob, and Joseph, Moses and David, and many other biblical characters who followed God. It was the reason for their courage because God said, "I will be with you wherever you go." It kept them going in dark times. It kept them encouraged in difficult times. That's why David declared in Psalm 23, "Yea though I walk through the valley of the shadow of death, I will fear no evil, for thou art with me."

We cannot live without the presence of the Lord. The omnipresence of God is the believer's security. God's glory and His indwelling presence is our lifeline. In the Old Testament Scriptures the glory of God manifested in the form of a cloud or fire, and when it appeared, people were healed, delivered, protected, and set free (Exodus 16:10 and 24:16-17). Throughout the gospels of the New Testament the glory of God manifested through Jesus (Matthew 16:27, Mark 13:26, and John 11). Since Jesus dwells in the believer, the glory of God also dwells in the believer.

In the Hebrew language the word *glory* means, "weighty, heavy, abundance, wealth, splendor, and honor." It was used in the Old Testament to describe a person's possessions, wealth, and abundance (Genesis 45:13). So what does this mean for us today? It means an invasion of wealth, abundance, and favor is in store for us.

I am so glad the Scripture verses in the Bible reassure us of Jesus' constant, abiding presence inside us. He doesn't just say it once and expect us to remember it. He says it repeatedly with the intention of getting it deep down in our souls, forever changing who we are and how we operate as children of the Most High.

- Deuteronomy 31:8 says, "The Lord himself goes before you and will be with you; He will never leave or forsake you. Do not be afraid; do not be discouraged."
- Hebrews 13:5 says, "Keep your lives free from the love of money, and be content with what you have, because God has said, "Never will I leave you; never will I forsake you."

- Deuteronomy 31:6, "Be strong and courageous. Do not be afraid or terrified because of them, for the Lord your God goes with you; he will never leave you nor forsake you."
- Joshua 1:5 says, "No one will be able to stand against you all the days of your life. As I was with Moses I will be with you; I will never leave you nor forsake you."
- First Chronicles 28:20 says, "David said to Solomon his son, 'Be strong and courageous. Do not be afraid or discouraged, for the Lord God, my God, is with you. He will not fail you or forsake you.'"
- John 14:18 say, "I will not leave you as orphans. I will come to you." (In this passage He has not yet ascended to the Father, so this is the promise of the Holy Spirit.)

Not only did He promise to always be with us, but there are 365 Scripture references that tell us in one way or another to "be not afraid." That's once for every single day of the year! There's no need for us to be tentative, isolated, or afraid when we choose to believe what God has said and when we walk as if it is so. We are mighty warriors who serve an awesome commander in chief.

$

Chapter 6

How then Should We See Ourselves?

Being human, we can often feel insignificant. Feelings of insecurity and insignificance are two of the greatest hindrances to our ability to receive what God has promised in His Word. In order to counter those feelings, we must choose to stop listening to the old tapes that run repeatedly through our minds. We've all experienced humiliation, failure, disappointment, and emotional wounds that make us feel unworthy and keep us living in defeat. That's why it's so essential that we choose to daily renew our minds by meditating on the Word of God, which explains in detail exactly how God feels about us.

Here is only a small sample describing what He says about His relationship with us:

- Romans 8:1 says, "There is therefore now no condemnation to those who are in Christ Jesus, who walk not after the flesh but after the spirit."
- Psalm 103:2 says, "Bless the Lord, O my soul, and forget not all his benefits. Who forgiveth all thine iniquities, who healeth all thy diseases; who redeemeth thy life from destruction, who crowneth thee with loving-kindness and tender mercies; who satisfieth thy mouth with good things, so that thy youth is renewed like the eagle's."

- Psalm 105:7 says, "He hath remembered His covenant forever, the word which he commanded to a thousand generations. Which covenant he made with Abraham, and his oath unto Isaac. And confirmed the same unto Jacob for a law, and to Israel for an everlasting covenant, saying, Unto thee will I give the land of Canaan, the lot of your inheritance—when they were but a few men in number; yea, very few, and strangers in it—when they went from one nation to another, from one kingdom to another people. He suffered no man to do them wrong; yea, he reproved kings for their sakes."
- Psalm 91:11 says, "For he shall give his angels charge over thee, to keep thee in all thy ways. They shall bear thee up in their hands, lest thou dash thy foot against a stone. Thou shalt tread upon the lion and the adder; the young lion and the dragon shalt thou trample underfoot. Because he hath set his love upon me, therefore will I deliver him, I will set him on high, because he hath known my name. He shall call upon me, and I will answer him; I will be with him in trouble; I will deliver him, and honor him. With a long life will I satisfy him and shew him my salvation."
- Second Corinthians 5:21 says, "For He hath made him to be sin for us, who knew no sin; that we might be made the righteousness of God in him."
- Romans 8:37 says, "We are more than conquerors through Him who loved us."
- John 14:12 says, "Verily, verily, I say unto you, He that believeth on me, the works that I do shall he do also; and greater works than these shall he do."
- Philippians 4:13 says, "I can do all things through Christ which strengthens me."
- Zechariah 2:8 says, "He that toucheth you toucheth the apple of his eye."
- Psalm 16:3 says, "To the saints that are in the earth, and to the excellent, in whom is all my delight."
- Second Timothy 1:7 says, "For God has not given us the spirit of fear, but of power, love and a sound mind."

- Isaiah 61:1 says, "I have anointed you to preach good tidings to the meek, to bind up the brokenhearted, to proclaim liberty to the captives, to open prison doors to those who are bound, to proclaim the acceptable year of the Lord, to comfort all that mourn."
- Zephaniah 3:17 says, "The Lord thy God, in the midst of thee is mighty; he will save. He will rejoice over thee with love, he will joy over thee with singing."
- Isaiah 60:1 says, "Arise, shine for thy light is come, and the glory of the Lord is risen upon thee."
- Isaiah 58:14 says, "And the Lord shall guide thee continually, and satisfy thy soul in drought, and make fat thy bones; and thou shalt be like a watered garden, and like the spring of water, whose waters fail not."
- Psalm 37:4 says, "Delight thyself in the Lord, and I will cause thee to ride on the high places of the earth, and feed thee with the heritage of Jacob."
- Psalm 1:1 says, "He shall be like a tree, planted by the rivers of water, whose leaf shall not wither, and whatsoever he doeth shall prosper."
- Matthew 7:7 says, "Ask what you will and it will be done unto you."
- James 1:6 says, "But when he asks he must believe and not doubt, because he who doubts is like a wave of the sea, blown and tossed by the wind."

And finally John 3:16, which says, "For God so loved _________ (put your name here) that He gave His only begotten Son, that whosoever believeth in Him should have eternal life." Are you grasping the incredible truth that God loved you so very much that He sent Jesus for you? Now if that isn't love, I don't know what is.

As we can clearly see, God is for us and has empowered us to rule the earth. But it's essential that we reach out and respond to His great love and walk passionately with our God.

One thing that tends to keep us off-kilter and feeling insecure and inadequate is when we compare ourselves with others. God made each of us so different that to compare ourselves with others is much like comparing apple with oranges. There really is no way they can be compared. And when you get right down to it, remember that when you compare yourself with someone else, you usually do it on your worst day against someone else's best day. In that case, you will never come out on top, so just choose to stop comparing yourself with others in the first place. God certainly doesn't compare you with anyone else . . . ever.

Does it surprise you to learn that God loves you for the special individual He made you to be—more than you could ever dream or imagine—and that He leans down, inclining His ear to hear your prayers? Do you believe it? Ask God to let mere head knowledge be transformed into heart knowledge, convincing you beyond a shadow of a doubt of His great love just for you. Then even when the Devil comes to say it isn't so, you will be able to stand on the truth of the Holy Scripture, which says otherwise.

$

Chapter 7

In Spite of Everything

I find it incredible that though God already knew ahead of time that they would sin, it didn't stop Him from creating His dream—Adam and Eve.

In fact, He was so delighted with them that the first words out of His mouth were blessings. And if, as Scripture says, God never changes, that means He still feels the same way about you and me. That blessing once again belongs to us because Jesus restored the blessing when He went to the cross and rose again, recapturing for us the dominion God imparted to mankind at creation.

Here's what the Bible says about that first blessing:

> So God created man in his own image, in the image of God created he him; male and female created he them. And God blessed them, and God said unto them, "Be fruitful, and multiply, and replenish the earth, and subdue it: and have dominion over the fish of the sea, and over the fowl of the air, and over every living thing that moveth upon the earth." (Genesis 1:27-28)

Here's a quote on this subject from author and speaker Kenneth Copeland's website:

> With those words, God imparted to Adam and Eve—and to all mankind—*THE BLESSING*. He told them who they were: the lords of the earth created by God in His image as rulers and royalty. He told them what they were supposed to do: replenish

> (or fill up) the earth, subdue it and bring it into line with the perfect will of God. He also gave them the power to carry out that assignment.

To *bless* actually means "to empower." So the first words Adam ever heard, the first sound that ever struck his eardrums was the sound of God's voice empowering him with the divine, creative ability to reign over the earth and make it a perfect reflection of God's best and highest will.

How did Adam know what God's perfect will for the earth was? All he had to do was look around him. He was living in the garden of Eden—a place created and ordered by God Himself. That garden was a perfect demonstration of God's plan for this planet. It was a prototype of what He wanted the whole thing to be.

Adam's job was to exercise his God-given authority and expand that garden until it encompassed the entire earth. That's what *the blessing* was for! It provided Adam with the power to carry on the work God began in creation. It equipped him with the divine resources he needed to follow God's example and, by speaking anointed, faith-filled words, transform the uncultivated parts of this planet into a veritable garden of Eden.

In other words, *the blessing* empowered Adam to be a blessing wherever he went. The garden of Eden was literally inside Adam. And it's inside you and me if we take it and move as if it is so.

Although Adam was empowered to be a blessing, he made several mistakes in his life. But whatever God permits, he permits for a reason. And His reasons are always infinitely wise and purposeful. He did not have to let the fall happen in Adam's life. He could have stopped it just like He could have stopped the fall of Satan. The fact that He did not stop it means He has a reason, a purpose for it. And He does not make up His plans as He goes along. What God knows to be wise He has always known to be wise. Therefore, Adam's sin and the fall of the human race with him into sin and misery did not take God off guard and is part of His overarching plan to display the fullness of the glory of Jesus Christ.

Adam messed up, but this is what grace is about. God's grace is more powerful than Adam's trespass and more powerful than your mistakes. That's what the words "much more" in Romans 5:20 signify. "Much more has the grace of God . . . abounded for many." If man's trespass brought death, will God's grace bring life? Paul said, "Much more have the grace of God and the free gift by *the grace of that one man Jesus Christ* abounded for many." These are not two different graces. "The grace of that one man Jesus Christ" is the incarnation of the grace of God. The grace that is in Jesus is the grace of God.

This grace is sovereign grace. It conquers everything in its path. It is reigning grace. That's why despite your past mistakes, past sins, past failures, past blunders, and past faults, God still blesses you. Despite everything you may have done against the will of God, God's grace wins. As a result, you receive blessings you don't deserve and didn't earn.

You should put this book down right now and celebrate the abounding grace of Christ—sovereign grace, God's grace.

$

Chapter 8

Heirs to a Fortune

Did you know that you and I are heirs to a fortune? We are heirs from the day we accepted the gift of salvation. That very day we were adopted into royalty, sons and daughters of a King who rules heaven and earth. That day we became heirs to a fortune so massive that it will take all of eternity to come to terms with what that means. We can trace our lineage all the way back to Abraham, Isaac, and Jacob, to whom God gave the blessing. And while we may not be related by blood, in the spirit we are truly their kin.

Everything God promised Abraham has become ours. The problem is that we have trouble getting a handle on such truth. The Bible tells us in Galatians 3:14, "That the blessing of Abraham might come on the Gentiles through Jesus Christ; that we might receive the promise of the Spirit through faith. And if ye be Christ's, then are ye Abraham's seed, and heirs according to the promise."

Now keep in mind that God's idea of a blessing is a far cry from what we as human beings believe. He doesn't just say a flippant "Bless you" when someone sneezes. Rather, He is actually conferring on us the power to increase and prosper in every area of our lives. In fact, according to both *Webster's Dictionary* and W. E. Vine, the word *bless* means "to cause to prosper, to make happy, to bestow favor upon, to consecrate to holy purposes, to make successful, to make prosperous in temporal concerns pertaining to this life, to guard and preserve."

When God blessed Abraham, He made him a rich man—rich not only in land but also in livestock, family, and finances. His herds actually increased in size so much that he and his nephew, Lot, had to go their separate ways because the grazing land was too crowded to support both men's herds.

God multiplied and blessed everything Abraham touched wherever he went. But the blessing wasn't limited to material things. It also applied to Abraham's ability to overcome every obstacle placed in his path. He was truly an overcomer, empowered because he walked in the blessing.

While Abraham's wealth was the result of the blessing of God, it was not the objective of God. God was not making a covenant with Abraham for the purpose of making him wealthy. It is often preached this way. God was making a covenant with Abraham for the purpose of bringing redemption to mankind. And the prosperity Abraham experienced was a benefit of his obedience to God. God clearly told Abraham that in receiving His blessing he was blessed to be a blessing. God was thinking about a lot more than Abraham. He was thinking about all of humanity. God was thinking about you. It is from Abraham that Christians receive God's blessings. After reading Abraham's story, here is what I believe:

- I believe God is about to break some things wide open for you and bless you beyond measure.
- I believe He is about to manifest Himself and bestow His manifold blessing upon you in a mighty way.
- I believe God is about to grant you plenty and bless all the work of your hand.
- I believe He has opened to you His good treasure and you will now lend and not borrow.
- I believe you are the head and not the tail. You are at the top even if it looks like you're at the bottom.
- I believe you're blessed in the city and blessed in the country.
- I believe you shall prosper in everything God has called you to do.
- I believe you are above and never will be beneath anything or anyone.

I believe God has commanded His blessing on you. It is a blessing, not a right. Don't get sidetracked. Don't get discouraged. Don't give up. Don't doubt God's Word. Don't let the Enemy rob you of your entitlement.

Do you believe God? Do you believe His Word? Do you believe what God has spoken over your life? Then you need to stand on His Word in the same way Abraham did, unmoved by time, unmoved by problems, and unmoved by circumstances that seem to drag on with no visible answers. Don't let any devil, demon, demonic force, person, or thing stop you from believing what God has promised you.

The blessing of Abraham belongs to you. You are an heir to a fortune, and I command you by the power of the Holy Ghost to live like you are entitled to what God has for you.

After looking at the life of Abraham, I'm convinced that there's no limit to what the blessing of God can do for anyone who dares to believe. The blessing plus our faith makes the impossible possible! That's why it's so important to remind ourselves of God's goodness to us in the past. If we don't see our promises coming as fast as we think they should, we need to bow to God's sovereignty, rest in His promise, and refuse to doubt, no matter what else happens. In the end, God has a great compensation plan for those who love and trust Him until the end.

Perhaps you've heard it said that the man who talks to himself is a little off? Well, in the case of believers, we need to talk to ourselves, giving ourselves pep talks and stirring up the embers of faith when they tend to die out from lack of fuel. That's the time when we need to pour fuel on that fire by reminding ourselves that God is God and His Word and His promises never fail. We need to preach to ourselves those truths we have heard and seen and the glory in recounting the wonderful things God has done to turn around for good what our Enemy meant for harm. For us, spiritual reruns are an excellent source of faith-building fuel, so replay every good thing God has done and share them with anyone else who will listen because it will be a word in season, like apples of gold, to hungry hearts that need to know God is real.

Recount the times when you were ready to give up but decided to take the need to God.

* * *

Not long ago a friend shared this story with me.

After several years of devastating losses she went into a deep depression from which she couldn't recover and eventually decided she could no longer live with the pain. What was the point when God seemed to have abandoned her? She had prayed and sought answers in God's Word, but she felt like her prayers were bouncing off the ceiling, the silence echoing to confirm her desperate state.

Having made up her mind to end her life, she made and froze meals, and she made arrangements so that her family could function without her. On a bright October day she got in her car and drove to a beautiful park divided by a railroad track. Though autumn was her favorite time of year she scarcely noticed the stunning landscape painted in dazzling fall colors by an unseen hand. At that point, instead of seeing its beauty, she only saw desolation wherever she looked because of the festering wounds in her heart.

It wasn't long before she could hear the distant vibration as the train rumbled down the track, shaking the ground beneath it. Her heart beat faster as she put the car into drive and pulled closer to the track, intending to drive onto it just before the train arrived.

Tears slid down her cheeks as she was hit by the harsh reality of death, which now stared her in the face. She didn't really want to die. She just wanted the pain to end because she couldn't face the heartache without the Lord, and for too long now He had been silent in answer to her cries. Didn't He care?

The train whistle blew, and she suddenly realized she had just enough time to pull onto the track; however, at that instant something stopped her. God appeared in the front passenger's seat in the form of a brilliant white light filled with warm compassion. She wept before He spoke a word, and then He said, "My dove, this is not My plan for you. I have long dreamed big dreams for you that you haven't yet seen. Nor can you even imagine them. And whether you believe it or not, I never left you. I am always here for you, so let's turn around and work on these things together."

That was all she needed to hear. He hadn't abandoned her. In fact, He was closer than ever, and that was enough to give her hope. Since that time He has used her in amazing ways, exactly as He told her He would, and she wants you, too, to know the truth of 1 Corinthians 2:9, which says, "Eye hath not seen, nor ear heard, that which God has planned for those who love Him."

We are all heirs to a fortune if only we take hold of it in faith and live as if it is so.

$

Chapter 9

Agreeing with God's Word

In order to break through to live and walk in the love and glory of God, we must see ourselves as God sees us and believe what He says about us, taking Him at His word. I like the familiar phrase that says, "I am who He says I am, and I can do what He says I can do." There is great power in transforming our thinking to agree with God's Word.

God gave us the Bible, which is His Word, His message to us. It is His operator's manual, given to man. God has made it perfectly clear who He is and what He wants. He is God. He wants us to believe Him and act with respect toward the fact that He is God. When we believe who God is, we will believe what God can do for us, through us, and in us.

We need to agree with God. When you get in agreement with God, then you are thinking the way that God thinks. You need to understand how God thinks so that you can get in agreement with Him.

Some of us unfortunately don't believe what the Word of God says about us, as indicated by our making statements that contradict what the Bible says. Instead of saying, "I can do all things through Christ, who strengthens me," we're saying, "I don't think I can make it." Such statements are what the Bible calls "bad reports" because they disagree with what God says (see Numbers 13:32). If, however, our hearts are full of God's Word, we will be full of faith, believing and saying only what agrees with the Holy Scripture.

When you come into agreement with God, you agree with God and everything He says and stands for. In other words, when you are in agreement with God, God will cause His Word to accomplish the purposes for which it has been released.

God is the God of the possible. Impossible is not found in His vocabulary, and impossibility doesn't exist in His universe. Everything is possible when you think the way God thinks. How does God think?

- **God thinks in abundance**. Jesus said that He had come so that you might have life and have it more abundantly.
- **God thinks in possibility**. All things are possible when you think the way God thinks. God is the God of possibility.
- **God thinks in positive expectations**. God expects good things to happen in your life when you think the way that He thinks. He says in Jeremiah 29:11, "My plans are for good and not for disaster, to give you a future and a hope."
- **God thinks about recovery of what has been lost**. What the world destroys and takes away God recovers and restores.
- **God thinks in favor**. He bestows His blessings on all who get in agreement with Him. He opens the windows of heaven, and blessings fall all around.

And His Word will not change or fail.

Powerful things happen when we come into agreement with God. When you confess what God's Word says about you, you are agreeing that what He said concerning you is true and will come to past. For example, consider the following:

- We must agree with God that He will bless us (Psalm 115:12).
- We must agree with God that all of our needs are supplied according to His riches in glory (Philippians 4:19).
- We must agree with God that He will increase us more and more even our children (Psalm 115:14).
- We must agree with God that we are already blessed of the Lord, who made heaven and earth (Psalm 115:15).

Jesus said in Mathews 18:19-20, "If two of you shall agree on earth as touching anything that they shall ask, it shall be done for them of My

Father which is in heaven. For where two or three are gathered together in My name, there am I in the midst of them." Many people believe that if two believers simply voice an agreement on anything, God is obligated to give them their request. This interpretation implies that the agreeing is the criteria, but that's not so. The only agreement God will answer is an agreement He agrees with. In other words, if two agree on anything according to the will of God, then God will answer. But if our request is not according to His will—that is, if God doesn't agree with us—then it doesn't matter how many believers we have in agreement with our request. God will not answer.

Agreement is harmony. Agreement is unity. Agreement with God is called confession, and confession is declaration. I challenge you to agree with God's Word. He wants you to agree and see His Word come to past in your life. So begin to say what God has said about you in His Word, the Holy Bible. Agree with God's Word, and His Word will begin to work for you!

Once we know the Word of God, we can be prepared to speak out loudly to those false messages of condemnation the Devil uses to haunt us and say, "No way! I refuse that negative message, Satan, because I am bought with a price, the precious blood of Jesus. Because I am in Christ, I am a new creation. Old things are passed away, and all things have become new, which means you can no longer accuse me of being the same loser kid who was mercilessly taunted and bullied in school. You can no longer accuse me of being the slow learner who failed eighth-grade geometry. You can no longer accuse me of anything in my past because it's dead along with my old identity. And when you remind me of my past, I'm going to remind you of your future. So be gone, Devil. You have no place in me . . . in Jesus' name!"

$

Chapter 10

Everything Jesus Has is Ours

You know, Jesus could've said to us, "Okay, guys. I've pulled you out of Satan's clutches, so now you'd better straighten up and fly right." But He didn't do that. He not only left His deity behind in heaven when He came to earth to redeem us with His own blood, but as we've already discovered, He also exalted us so that we are joint heirs with Christ Jesus, adopting us into His family so that we don't merely live as slaves but are actually heirs of the covenant promises God made to Adam and Abraham. In other words, everything Jesus has is ours! Hallelujah!

Far too often we strive to work even harder in depending on ourselves and earthly others, retreating even further from our Father. But such a mentality is incorrect. All that the Father has is ours. God has already given us everything we need so we can prosper in all areas of our lives. We just need to learn to recognize this. God is greater than any lack you can ever have, and when we begin to focus on God being greater in us, the lack shrinks by leaps and bounds.

The more we appreciate and acknowledge what God gives us, the less we notice what might appear to be lacking. John 17:10 says "All that I have is yours." This is the fullness of God's promise: "All that the Father has is mine." Second Peter 1:3 says, "According as His divine power hath given unto us all things that pertain unto life and godliness, through the knowledge of Him that hath called us to glory and virtue." In His wisdom and grace God has seen to it that we have everything we need to produce "life and godliness."

Everything that we have is a gift. We must have that attitude. We must remember that God has blessed us. None of us earned our blessings. None of us continues to earn favor. It's all a gift from God. None of us can earn favor or blessings, and if we think we've earned it, you've made a mistake.

We underestimate what God has given us. The world itself and all the blessings that are on our earth, God gave that to us. We never made it or earned it. Our abilities and everything we have is a gift from God.

We have to have the attitude that I don't own what God has given to me. It's God's gift. I haven't earned it. I can't earn it. It's a gift from God. So when it comes to our material goods, how do we avoid greed? I think it starts with that attitude that all that I have doesn't really belong to me. It belongs to God.

What do you give the God who has everything? Nothing! You can't give God anything! It's already His! God, by definition, owns everything. It all comes from Him and belongs to Him. God is the source of everything that exists. All things come to us by means of the channels of blessing He has established for us.

God wants us to prosper in every area of our lives, and when it comes to the monetary, He said to not worship or love money, but He didn't say to not have any to live. It is God's will that his people prosper. In Mathew 7:11, Jesus was very clear when he said, "How much more will your Father in heaven give good gifts to those who ask him." Jesus is making it clear that all good things come from heaven, and that having prosperity is a gift from heaven, and heaven-sent. Jesus wants us to have heaven-sent prosperity and the Bible is packed with scriptural insights on this subject. Here are a few scriptures that will increase your faith and change the way you think about heaven-sent prosperity:

- John 16:15 (NLT) says, "All that the Father has is mine; this is what I mean when I say that the Spirit will reveal to you whatever he receives from me."
- Ephesians 1:3 (NLT) says, "How we praise God, the Father of our Lord Jesus Christ, who has blessed us with every spiritual blessing in the heavenly realms because we belong to Christ."

- Ephesians 1:6 (NLT) says, "So we praise God for the wonderful kindness he has poured out on us because we belong to his dearly loved Son."
- Joshua 6:16 (KJV) says, "Shout ; for the LORD hath given you the city."
- Matthew 16:19 (KJV) says, "And I will give unto thee the keys of the kingdom of heaven: and whatsoever thou shalt bind on earth shall be bound in heaven: and whatsoever thou shalt loose on earth shall be loosed in heaven."
- Mark 9:41 (KJV) says, "Because ye belong to Christ, verily I say unto you, he (you) shall not lose his (your) reward."

Many of us have been Christians for a long time and know those Scriptures backward, forward, and upside down, but we have yet to put them into practice and act on them as if they are the truth. At this point let me make it clear that God wants us to have a much broader view of things. He wants us to repent for our unbelief and let go of the old slave mentality that keeps us in fear, timid and indecisive, continually unsure of ourselves. He wants us to see ourselves in a new light, forgetting those things that are behind us, whatever they are, and beginning to walk into our destiny as anointed hands and feet of God. He has given us authority and dominion to do greater things than Jesus did, but in order for that to happen, we must stop groveling and seeing ourselves through tainted eyes of failure and defeat. We must also stop fearing Satan because he, too, was put under our feet when Jesus stripped him of power. Colossians 2:15 tells the whole story. When He disarmed the rulers and authorities, He made a public display of them, having triumphed over them through Him.

Answer this question: "Do I often question the will of God for me, knowing He *can* do what I ask but unsure that He will? If that describes you, it's time to end the questions and stand in confidence, believing God *does want* to answer your prayers and bless you.

With that in mind, we must fill our minds with the truth about the power we have in Christ and His Word. We must step out to take hold of our destiny as never before. It's at that point that we can speak His Word to our storms and our needs and tell them to come under authority. That's why, as children of the King, we are instructed to come boldly without shame or apology and make known our requests to God, who wants nothing more than to demonstrate His glory when He answers them.

Here's an exercise that will change your life if you implement it:

Did you know that you never have to have another down day the rest of your life, that you can rise above all negative emotions and put them under your feet forever?

Here's how: Visualize all the negative emotions as things you can stuff in a large duffel bag. See yourself setting that bag in a chair across from you. Then speak to the negative emotions. Say, "You know, Jesus told me you were coming, but He took you all to the cross and then rose from the grave, shattering depression, sadness, desperation, loneliness, and every other negative emotion I could ever have so that I could put you under my feet and be victorious over you. Therefore, I tell you to be gone in the name of Jesus, for the joy of the Lord is my strength. Hallelujah!"

In the same way you talk to negative emotions, you can talk to pain and sickness of any kind because your body is the temple of the Holy Spirit and He has given you dominion over anything that hinders its function. So you tell your pain, "In Jesus' name, I put you under my feet and declare that you must leave right now because you have been defeated on the cross, never to haunt me again." If the Devil returns with pain symptoms once you have prayed, just stand on the truth of your healing and continue to reject the Devil's lies.

Oh, and one more thing—

Let me remind you that you are a top priority in God's mind. No matter how things look or how you feel, God has not forgotten you. No matter how many people have let you down and how badly you may have failed, He remembers you in your weakest, most vulnerable moments. The next time you feel helpless and hopeless or desperate, God will be there for you, so call on His name for help. At that point if you can say nothing else, whisper His name because there's power in the name of Jesus. And whether you can feel it or not, know this: He had a very good plan in mind when He created you.

For those of you who felt rejected as children, unwanted, abused, or abandoned by those who should've loved you most, take heart because in His deep compassion God has heard your cries and felt your deep, unrelenting pain and He's reaching out to you now right where you are.

He says, "Come unto Me, all you who are weary and heavy-laden, and I will give you rest. Take My yoke upon you, and learn of Me, for I am meek and lowly in heart, and ye shall find rest for your souls. For my yoke is easy and my burden is light."

Not long ago the Lord showed me that the hindrances and wounds of the past are much like a rusty, dirty filter through which we see and feel everything, coloring our perceptions. I think that's what 1 Corinthians 13:12 means when it says, "For now we see in a glass darkly, but then face to face."

As a result, we can't experience what God wants to show or tell us apart from that tainted, negative influence. And now because time is short and He wants us to rise up and walk in power, He wants our permission to touch and heal them so that they no longer influence the way we receive from God.

A friend recently shared a vision in which God showed her the picture of a long, running scar with the tracks of a terrible, jagged wound sown with thick black suture thread. It was ugly, and it made her cringe just to look at it. It had to have been the result of terrible trauma. In a second picture He showed her a naked newborn baby lying on its tummy on a blanket. He let her see that He wanted to touch her wounds and make them brand new just like that smooth, shiny baby's skin, with every scar completely healed. It's only when we are restored that we are able to see and hear with the eyes and ears of faith, unhindered by the hurts of the past. Only then can we reflect the marvelous glory He wants to pour through us.

At this point I'd like to give you a heads-up that will help you succeed no matter what you're going through. Your feelings are the Devil's playground, and he will use them to drag you around by the neck like a dog wearing an overly tight collar. He will take you down the road to depression and despair if you let him, convincing you that you are inadequate and never good enough to be worthy of God's love. That's why you need to put your feelings under your feet, believing and declaring only what God's Word says about you.

It's okay to admit your feelings to God, but then dump them at the foot of the cross and admit the truth, saying, "Listen, Lord, I can't handle these things. So I dump them in Your lap and declare that I have forgiven and shed every offense and stand on the Word of God, which says I was created in God's image, bought with a price, the precious blood of Jesus, and now am a brand-new creation. God has also given me the authority to subdue every feeling that doesn't line up with what His Word says, so I refuse to let these feelings keep me from living in the glory."

Regarding opinions that rise from emotions, we all have them, but we need to remember that they, too, are filtered through our damaged filters. If we care to check out God's opinions on those issues, we can easily see that our deeply held and personally defining opinions are often miles apart from the way God see things. The question we have to ask ourselves here is this: "Just because I've always felt this way, am I going to continue to hold onto my old, stubborn opinions, or am I ready to let God make them new as well?"

When Peter was with Jesus in the garden of Gethsemane, he cut off the ear of the high priest, believing he was defending Christ (John 18:10-11). But how did Jesus respond? He rebuked Peter, telling him to put his sword back in its sheath, and then He restored the man's ear, probably making Peter feel like an idiot. Why? Because his behavior was out of sync with the plan of God for Jesus' life. In the same way you and I need to ask God how He sees and feels about things and then adjust our opinions accordingly if we don't want to be out of the will of God.

In that regard, I once did a word study of Luke 14, where it says, "If any man comes to me and does not hate his father, and mother and brothers and sisters he cannot be my disciple." By that He meant that once we know the truth about Christ and have tasted and walked in freedom and power, we cannot be His disciples if we return to our old ways instead of leaving them behind. If we continue to wallow in our wounds and old, negative emotions and offenses, refusing to let them go, or if we take them up again once we've let them go, we refuse to be His disciples.

Envision this: He wants to hold you in His lap and snuggle you against His chest so that you can hear His very heartbeat and you will understand the yearnings of His heart and get in line with His plan.

Not long ago another friend shared this vision. The Lord came to her early in the morning and began to pull off what looked like leeches from her skin. He said they were offenses, wounds that had colored her outlook so that she couldn't see clearly with the eyes of faith. In effect, they were dimming the glory He wanted to shine through her. When she woke from the vision, several offenses and wounds from past rejection had lost their power. She was healed! Ask God to reveal the areas that are still hindering you from walking in the glory. Ask Him to show you areas where you haven't yet let go of the old in order to walk in newness of life.

For years I thought I was the source of the negative emotions in my mind. And while they could've arisen out of negative life experiences, the Lord showed me that the Devil was the source, and because his goal is to steal, kill, and destroy, he will whisper discouraging words and condemnation that only bring us down. Remember, God has forgotten those things, and if your mind is as new as the new creation you are, those thoughts are not from you, so put the blame right where it belongs and defend yourself with words of authority, putting the Devil under your feet.

If you experience times when you question God's love, just know that those notions are also lies whispered by the Enemy, who knows that until we are completely secure and confident in the love of God, we cannot walk in power and victory the way God intends us to. To counter those lies, we must meditate on the Holy Scripture and decree and declare to the Enemy what God's Word says about us.

* * *

God actually likes you! Perhaps that's a new thought, but He does . . . absolutely. Maybe you've assumed that God only obligated Himself to love you because you accepted His gift of salvation. Nothing could be further from the truth. He designed you before the creation of the earth. You were born in His imagination, the result of His creative genius long before your actual physical birth, and He loves and delights in you. Ask any author, designer, or inventor, and he will tell you he enjoys and admires (sets his deep affection on) his inventions.

In the same way, when God finished His creation, He looked at all He had created (no doubt smiling at that point) and said that it was good! That includes you and me.

$

Chapter 11

The High Cost of Doubt

Right now you may be thinking, *What's the big deal? Everyone has doubts now and then about faith.* While that may be true, it doesn't please God because we are either living in faith or in doubt, which is nothing more than unbelief. And living that way actually prevents us from receiving the blessings God intended because our unbelief opens the door to Satan, giving him a legal right to steal from us.

James 1:5-8 puts it this way: "But if any of you lacks wisdom let him ask of God, who gives to all men generously, and without reproach, and it will be given to him. But let him ask in faith, for the one who doubts is like the surf of the sea, driven and tossed by the wind. For let not that man expect that he will receive anything from the Lord, being a double-minded man, unstable in all his ways."

Not long ago I heard from a woman who said she had been praying fervent, diligent prayers, asking God to move on her behalf. After I questioned her further, however, I discovered that she had been praying out of fear rather than faith. She needed to believe she had received title deed to her answer the moment she prayed and then choose to stand in faith instead of in fear.

Answer the following questions: Did you have to work or strive or beg and plead for your salvation? No, because it's a free gift. Did you have to sweat and struggle to earn the baptism of the spirit? No, because once again it's a gift. What about your healing? Did you have to work to earn it?

The same answer applies when we ask God for His blessings. God says that whatever we ask in faith, He will do with no stress, no begging, and no sweat, so when it's all said and done, we simply need to believe it's so the moment we pray. That means when someone prays for us, we respond with the words, "I believe I receive!" Then we can rest and say, "It is finished."

On a related matter, did you know that God doesn't move in response to need the way we often do? If He did, we wouldn't have any needs, would we? No, He responds only to faith.

As human beings, our emotions so often motivate us that we need to be careful about simply being motivated by needs. Instead we need to seek God's wisdom to know whether a need is something He wants us to address. Once again Jesus is our example. He only did what His Father told Him to do. Why should we be any different? If we don't want to burn out, we need to move in response to God's instructions and not rely on our own wisdom.

Believe it or not, doubt can have life-and-death consequences. Recently I heard the true story of a three-year-old boy who drowned in his backyard swimming pool. A neighbor lady who was a Christian grabbed her husband and ran to the rescue after she heard the terrified screams of the mother. As they began CPR on the little guy, the woman turned to her husband, who looked doubtfully at the blue, lifeless body of the child, and under her breath, she whispered, "Don't you dare say a word." Then she began to pray and speak over that child that he would live and not die in order to declare the works of the Lord. She praised God that the child was going to be fine with no brain damage or other ill effects. Momentarily the rescue unit arrived and shortly whisked away the lifeless child.

When they arrived at the hospital twenty minutes later, the mother was shocked to hear the doctor say, "We've never seen anything like it. He was flat line, with no pulse or respirations whatsoever in the ambulance, but only moments later he suddenly woke up and said he was hungry. He's fine. You can take him home whenever you're ready."

The neighbor later told her husband, "If any of us had said a single word of doubt, that baby would be dead this instant, but he's alive!" We dare not entertain doubt for a single second or speak what we see with our eyes because our doubt will cancel out faith every time!

Desperation: The Greatest Motivation for Bad Choices

Have you ever noticed that desperate people do desperate things? They rob banks and stoop to identity theft, embezzlement, or even premeditated murder, to name only a few. Have you ever been desperate enough to do something unwise? A friend said that during a time when her husband was unemployed, she went online and responded to some "work at home" business propositions. But instead of making any money, it cost her hundreds of nonrefundable dollars because few of the opportunities were actually legitimate. Rather than running to the Lord with their needs, she chose to make something happen in the natural, and as always it ended badly.

So what should we do in such situations? Once again we look to Jesus as our example. He always did exactly what His Father said. He never just ran out and made something happen, even though He had many opportunities to do that. Instead even when the need was great, He waited until He could get away and ask God for wisdom. And God always met the need of the moment.

In the same way you and I should consult God. However, if you're like most of us, especially in the United States, you tend to go into overdrive, feeling a quirky sense of urgency instead of holding your peace until you can get God's take on it. That's because we've been programmed with a work ethic that says it's better to do anything than to do nothing at all. Can you see how counter that is to the will of God?

God's will is that we stop, quiet our hearts, ask for wisdom, and then get in line with that plan and move in sync with the Holy Spirit. At that point we will see supernatural intervention because God is behind it, and our situations will turn around for our good.

In Mark 11:15-19, we find Jesus in the temple, where money changers were buying and selling as if they were in a noisy and chaotic bazaar. And while we may assume that His assignment that day was to clean house, overturning the tables in the temple, that wasn't really the point. He went there to preach the Gospel, and the money changers would have distracted the people, making His preaching ineffective. I find it interesting that the first time He walked into the temple that day He did nothing, even though

He instantly saw the problem. Instead He found a quiet place to pray and then went back to do what His Father said.

Now keep in mind that when Jesus came to earth, He left His deity behind and actually lived just as we do, in a limited human body with a limited human mind. That's exactly why He needed to consult His Father.

The point is that we, too, need to get into the habit of quieting our hearts and stifling that sense of urgency and then consulting God instead of moving in our flesh to make something happen. If we make God our source of wisdom and do only what our Father says, we will no longer find it necessary to rush into things in a panic or do the wrong thing. Let's get in the habit of waiting on the Lord and watch how He turns everything around!

In good times or bad, we should focus on the Lord and His good plan for our lives. We'll save ourselves much grief in the end if we stay the course instead of running off on our own.

Don't Doubt It

Jesus placed a greater blessing on those who believe without seeing than those who believe because they have seen. In other words, there is a greater anointing on believing the Word than believing signs and wonders. John 20:29 reads, "Jesus saith unto him, Thomas, because thou hast seen me, thou hast believed: blessed are they that have not seen, and yet have believed." There is a greater blessing on just believing God's Word than there is on believing because of supernatural circumstances.

The word *doubt* means a status between belief and disbelief, and it involves uncertainty or distrust or a lack of sureness of an alleged fact. In this case, the alleged fact is the written Word of God. Doubt is not simply intellectual. Nor is it merely psychological. Doubt is personal. It is a matter of truth, trust, and trustworthiness. Can we trust God? Do we trust Him enough to depend on Him utterly?

We must comprehend that God is not only a person but a supreme person on whom all personhood depends. God is more certain and more faithful than our doubting views of Him. That is why to know Him is to trust Him and to trust Him is to begin to know ourselves. As a follower of Christ, we must trust and believe that God will do exactly what His word says He will do.

Understand that *doubt* is not sinful, but it can be dangerous. It can also be a spur to enormous spiritual growth. It's what you do with your doubt that matters. That's why you should always aim to doubt your doubts, not your faith. This simply means that you should not cast away your faith simply because you are in the deep valley of darkness. All of us walk into that valley from time to time. Some of us spend a great deal of time there. But when you find yourself in that valley where all is uncertain and you are sorely tempted to give in to your doubts, fears, and worries, remember these two words: "Believe God!"

My friend, if you have made a decision to doubt or be uncertain about God's Word, then it's time to make a decision to have faith in God. To believe in God demands an act of faith, as does the decision not to believe in Him. What will it be? Faith or doubt? The choice is yours.

$

Chapter 12

Don't Worry

The gospel of Matthew talks about anxiety. Jesus, the Messiah, tells us in the sixth chapter of Matthew to "take therefore no thought for the morrow: for the morrow shall take thought for the things of itself" (Matthew 6:34). In other words, take no thought about life's basic needs. Do not become so anxious or disturbed about material needs that you start distrusting God. The bottom line is that you shouldn't worry about something that God has promised to provide. The implication of the text is that all anxiety is provoked by worrying about material and temporary things. So Jesus said, "Take no thought about tomorrow."

We cannot help but be deeply challenged by Jesus' words. On one hand, we hear Jesus saying, "Don't worry," and we think, *C'mon, Jesus, it was so easy for you. No wife and no kids to worry about, no office hours to keep, no bills to pay.* But on the other hand, isn't there something deeply attractive here, an invitation to a life that is not filled with unnecessary anxiety, stress, and fruitless worry? However, we can live in the way that Jesus describes.

In the twenty-first century it seems that human beings are worriers by our very nature. Whether it's those big global things, the basic personal things, or even things we consider to be important but other people would consider silly, we worry. And if that wasn't enough, we even worry about worrying.

Doesn't it seem odd that we take up so much time and energy with worry and anxiety? When we step back and think with our heads rather than our hearts, we know that worrying is futile. But worry and anxiety is an emotion closely related to fear, a basic survival instinct.

When we look at the words *anxiety*, *stress*, *fear*, and *tension*, technically these words have different meanings, but they are all used to describe one of the most prevalent characteristic in society. When you deal with anxiety, stress, and tension, you're speaking about one of the most urgent problems of our day. Everybody is uptight, anxious, and in a hurry. It has been suggested that an average person's anxiety is focused in the following ways:

- Forty percent on things that will never happen.
- Thirty percent on things about the past that can't be changed.
- Twelve percent on criticism by others, most of which is untrue.
- Ten percent on health, which gets worse with stress.
- And only 8 percent about real problems that we will face.

Webster's American English Dictionary defines anxiety as "an inner feeling of apprehension or an uneasiness; a concern and a worry; a sort of dread that is accompanied by heighten physical arousal." Anxiety has been identified as one of the official emotions of our age. It is an inordinate or solicitous concern or grief beyond our immediate need. It is the direct opposite of faith.

Anxiety has come upon all of us. It is the greatest single problem that exists among men. People of every race and color are worried and scared to some degree because of anxiety.

Let's take a look at the stages of worry that are acute, chronic, neurotic, and normal.

When you talk about acute anxiety, it comes quickly, and it is of high intensity. All of sudden you're thrown in a situation where your heart goes fast like you are driving down the freeway. Somebody moves in your lane and almost hits your car. You swerve your car over quickly and call on Jesus at the same time. Your heart goes fast, but quickly you're up. But thank God you settle down again. Acute anxiety is when behavior changes in the individual, and it is generally following a panic attack. It is characterized by panic attacks that are brought on because of sudden and excessive fear.

Chronic anxiety is the state of being anxious and tense all the time. It is the response to emotional pressure suffered for a prolonged period over which an individual perceives he or she has no control. The person is always worrying, with something on his or her mind that seems to pull the individual down into low depression. I believe the psalmist David ran into this when he looked down within himself and said, "Soul why has thou disquieted within me" (Psalm 43:5). Haven't you been there—just upset and beset and you don't even know what is causing you to be emotionally distressed and disappointed. Sometimes you have had to ask yourself the following questions:

- Am I a child of God, or aren't I?
- Does God love me, or doesn't He?
- Is my God able, or isn't He?

It is at this stage of your Christian walk that you must believe that God is so big, so strong, and so mighty that there is nothing He cannot do.

Next we deal with normal anxiety, which is defined as the real threat or situation that comes upon us that is proportionate. In other words, the anxiety within us responds equivalent to the problem. You do not become more anxious than what there is cause for. There are some situations that cause anxiety, but we must make sure our levels stays normal. This is what God is telling us: "We ought not to react more to a situation than you need to because that brings about an abnormal or neurotic anxiety."

Neurotic anxiety carries with it more fear than is necessary, which brings an exaggerated feeling of helplessness even when the danger is mild or nonexistence. No wonder Jesus said, "Sufficient to the day is the evil thereof." The word *sufficient* means "enough to meet the needs of a situation." Jesus wanted us to understand that each day had its own troubles and challenges. And that we should live in the present without a care for tomorrow.

Worry affects our total being. Worry doesn't change anything. Worry produces no profitable results. Worrying is a dead-end street. It goes nowhere. If you're not careful, worrying can become a way of life. It gives you a false sense of importance, as if to say that by worrying you're somehow making a difference.

Worry is so common to man. The young and old, the rich and poor, the learned and unlearned, the saints and sinners, and the faithful and unfaithful all have worries. We worry about our money, how we are going to get it, keep it, and spend it.

Worrying never lifted a single burden. It never dried a single tear. It never solved a single problem. Worry is faithless. Worry indicates a weakness in our faith. Jesus describes one that worries by saying, "O ye of little faith" (Matthew 6:30). Do we not have faith that God will be with us and those whom we worry about? We need not become of doubtful mind and worry about what may happen, for whatever did happen may be for our good. The apostle Paul said, "All things work together for good to them that love God" (Romans 8:28). Could it be, brethren, that we really do not have true faith in God?

This is why *worry* was important enough for Jesus to talk about it. Jesus said, "Therefore I say to you, do not worry about your life" (Matthew 6:25). Jesus is commanding us to cease from worry or anxiety. The Greek word that is here translated *worry* (*merimnaō*) is actually a word that can mean more than the negative idea of anxiety. It means "to be concerned" or "careful" for something in a broad sense, and it is often used for *care* in a perfectly good way.

As Jesus observed, we have a perennial tendency to worry not just about today but tomorrow as well. Mark Twain said, "I have spent most of my life worrying about things that have never happened." The problem for many Christians is not knowing what will happen tomorrow, which creates anxiety today.

God wants you to know that when you worry, you are living in perpetual insecurity. If God can take care of the birds and the lilies through the normal process of nature. He can certainly take care of you. Didn't His word say, "Behold the fowls of the air: for they sow not, neither do they reap, nor gather into barns; yet your heavenly Father feedeth them. Are ye not much better than they" (Matthew 6:26)?

One example of the things we should not worry about is food (Matthew 6:25-26). It is pointed out that fowls, which don't sow, reap, or gather, are fed by the heavenly Father. So why should we constantly worry about our eatables since we are obviously better than the fowls? Yet another example that Jesus gives is our raiment (Matthew 6:28-30). We are urged to consider the lilies of the field, which neither toil nor spin, yet even Solomon in all of his glory was not arrayed like one of these. So why should we be anxious and worry about our clothing since we are much better than the grass of the field?

You are valuable to God. You are His child, and He takes care of His own. In writing to the Christians at Philippi, Paul urged them to "be careful for nothing" (Philippians 4:6). Other versions render that phrase as follows: "In nothing be anxious." Paul is warning Christians against a fretful and feverish attitude toward life. "Do not engage in anxious thought" is simply what the apostle is saying.

Worrying is not good for you. It will only weigh you down and become a mental burden that could cause you to grow physically sick. Here's a little formula to remember: Worry replaced by prayer equals trust and removes fear.

$

Chapter 13

Lord, I Believe

Now that I'm older, I am much more comfortable with the idea that there are some things about God that I will never fully understand. And through this inability to know everything about God, I have learned something important about the nature of God. If I understood everything about God and could give answers to the most simple and the most complex questions about God, then He wouldn't be God. I say that because God is greater, more powerful, more mysterious, and even more loving than I could ever imagine or explain or describe to another human. I have a college degree, but still I don't have the words to describe the greatness and majesty and grace of God. I am experienced only in things of this world, and there is nothing in this world with which I can compare God.

To explain God, I have to fit Him in my frame of reference. I have to be able to comprehend what it means to be God. I need to have words that are able to describe something that is right outside of anything I experience in this world. It's easy to come up with formulas and explanations about God, but to do that, I have to hem Him in and restrict Him only to what I can understand. And as soon as I do that, God is no longer the God of majesty, power, and grace but something less than all that because I can't comprehend anything greater than my own world of experience.

So one of the first things I have to do is recognize that there is something mysterious and unknown about God. And as soon as I become used to the concept that there is something mysterious about God, then I have no problem saying, "I don't know some things about God." But just because I don't know some things about God, it does not mean I don't believe in God.

Let's revisit the word "believe." The word *believe* means "to accept as true or take to be true; to be confident about something." The word *believe* is given a lot of airtime in the Scriptures. It's a word that we would do well to look into with more detail. Some equate *belief* or *believe* with faith. However, the two are not synonymous. They're not the same.

In the Hebrew the word *believe* is *aman.* It means "to support, confirm, be faithful, uphold, nourish, to be established, be carried, make firm, stand firm, to trust, to be certain, or to believe in." That's nothing unusual or new to you necessarily. In the Greek the word is *pisteuo*, and it is translated as believe. It means "to think to be true, to be persuaded of, to credit, place confidence in." It means to trust in Jesus or God as able to aid either in obtaining or in doing something.

We all have doubts. We all have disbelief. This is common, and Jesus understands this. But if there is anything Christians need to ponder and experience anew, it is the power of God's Word, for only when we seize and are seized by the Word of God do we know the exceeding greatness of His power toward us who believe (Ephesians 1:19).

Hebrews 11:6 declares that "without faith it is impossible to please him, for those who come to him must believe that he is and that he is a rewarder of those who diligently seek him." So faith is responding to the revelation of God and to the Word of God. It doesn't get any plainer than that. This Scripture is the only real foundation worth establishing your life on.

There is a big difference between believing in God and believing God. Believing in God is not a drug to sedate you through life but a force to transport you to another realm of reality. Believing means accepting all of Jesus' teaching. For instance, you will accept the following:

- After miraculously feeding five thousand men plus women and children with five loaves of bread and two small fish, the disciples gathered up twelve baskets of leftover food (John 6:5-13). Then those men, when they had seen the sign that Jesus did [the miracle of feeding the multitude], said, "This is truly the Prophet who is to come into the world" (John 6:14)—a reference to a great successor to Moses foretold in the Holy Scripture. These men believed that Jesus truly was of God.

- After Jesus departed from the scene, many of those who enjoyed the miraculous meal came searching for Him. They wanted Jesus to perform another miracle, saying that this would help them believe Him (John 6:30).
- Rather than perform another miracle at this time, Jesus taught the people. He explained that unlike the physical bread the crowd had recently eaten, He was the true bread from heaven who would give eternal life to the world (John 6:32-33).
- He told them that His followers would need to "eat the flesh of the Son of Man and drink His blood" (John 6:53), referring to the symbols of bread and wine in the annual Passover service and internalizing what these meant, affirming their covenant relationship with Him. This would ultimately lead to eternal life (John 6:54).
- Many of those listening to Jesus, including His own disciples, found this teaching difficult to understand (John 6:60). Addressing this large group, Jesus then said, "But there are some of you who do not believe." Jesus knew from the beginning who they were who did not believe and who would betray Him. After this, "Many of His disciples went back and walked with Him no more" (John 6:64, 66).

Though many of these same people had said that they believed Jesus was the Prophet whose coming was foretold by Scripture (John 6:14), they did not believe what Jesus said. What Jesus meant by believing in Him *included believing everything He said*. It meant far more than just accepting free gifts He was offering. Again we must believe everything that God has said about Himself. Losing belief in the promises of God can cause those promises to be taken away. In Numbers 20:12 we find these words: "And the LORD spake unto Moses and Aaron, Because ye believed me not, to sanctify me in the eyes of the children of Israel, therefore ye shall not bring this congregation into the land which I have given them."

Then the Lord spoke to Moses and Aaron. "Because you did not believe Me, to hallow Me in the eyes of the children of Israel, therefore you shall not bring this congregation into the land which I have given them."

To believe is a commandment, a commanded belief. Did you know that? First John 3:29 reads, "Jesus answered and said to them: 'This is the work of God, that you believe in Him whom He sent. This is His commandment: that you should believe on the name of His Son Jesus Christ and love one another as He gave us commandment.'"

We're commanded to believe in our Savior. We're commanded to believe in Him, Christ, whom He, the Father, sent. It's part of our job description. It's part of our work description. It's commanded. We are commanded to believe in the name of Jesus Christ.

So what does "believe in God" mean? We say, "I have always believed in God." My question is this: Are you certain that you do? We believe in our problems, our setbacks, our troubles, and our hurts because we cry over them, complain about them, and have pity parties concerning test and trails. But are you certain that you believe in God?

Do you believe that God is eternity to eternity, the absolute and the eternal one? Do you believe that God is from everlasting to everlasting? Do you believe that He is light and dark, a consuming fire? Do you believe that God is life and the air you breathe? Do you believe that He is everything, that He knows everything, that He is the maker of everything and has brought everything into being? Do you really believe that He is present everywhere? Do you believe that He is omniscient and omnipresent? Do you believe that nothing happens apart from Him, apart from His sight, and without His knowledge? Do you believe that He is the originator, the architect; the author, the Creator of everything that is and is to come? Do you believe that He is almighty and all-powerful? Do you believe that He controls everything, directs everything and everybody? Finally do you believe that He is able to do everything and anything? Then believe in God and have faith in Him.

So the question now is this: "How do I have faith in God?" Allow me to borrow from Romans 10:17. It says, "Faith cometh by hearing and hearing by the word of God." If "faith cometh by hearing," then there has to be credibility in the presentation of the person talking in order for me to believe the person speaking. I have to believe God in order for me to hear God. I have to believe what God is speaking to me in order for me to hear what God is saying.

When I hear God, I have to imagine or visualize in my mind the God that I'm hearing about. I have to visualize in my mind the Word of God coming from God so that it can trigger in my heart the conception of God and cause me to believe in a God that I have heard about but have never seen. The moment I do this, I have disconnected the operation of God from anything that is connected to my senses. Once that happens, I have stepped over into faith, and my faith helps me to believe in a God whom I can't see with my eyes.

Faith is trusting God even when you have no visible, physical, or tangible evidence to support your decision. Faith is following when you don't know when, believing when you don't know how, and trusting when you don't know why.

Faith is the upholder, the foundation of things hoped for, and the evidence of things that aren't seen. In other words, I believe God for something that I don't see with my eyes, but I already see it because I perceive it with my faith. And the things I perceive with my faith are just as real as the things I see with my eyes because my faith tells me what I see in my spirit is coming to pass if I believe God.

In Mark 9:23 it reads, "Jesus said unto him, If thou canst believe, all things are possible to him that believeth." Do you see what God is saying to you? Anybody who does not have faith does not have a title to anything. That's why the writer declared in Hebrews 11:6, "Without faith it is impossible to please God." That's why the word of God encourages us to do the following:

- Walk by faith, not by sight (2 Corinthians 5:7).
- Above all, taking the shield of faith (Ephesians 6:16).
- Let us hold fast the confession of faith (Hebrews 10:23).
- The just shall live by faith (Hebrews 10:38).
- This is the victory that overcometh the world even our faith (1 John 5:4).

So if I don't have anything from God, it is because I didn't believe God for anything. If I don't have anything, it is because I didn't believe God for something. But with faith everything is possible. So believe in God. When you do, the following is possible:

- It's possible to have divine favor.
- It's possible to have material wealth
- It's possible to walk in prosperity.
- It's possible to live in blessings.
- It's possible to have doors open.
- It's possible to have ways made.
- It's possible for God to enlarge your territory
- It's possible for God to bless you and give you more.
- It's possible for you to have more than you need.
- It's possible for the contract to be signed and for the money to roll in.
- It's possible to have a bigger house—and live in one—that you did not build.
- It's possible to experience a land flowing with milk and honey.
- It's possible to get a better car and a better church, to get a husband, or to get a wife.
- It's possible to be healed, to be delivered, and/or to be set free.
- It's possible to be blessed in the city and to be blessed in the field.
- It's possible for your son to get off crack and for your daughter to be saved.
- It's possible for the vision to come to pass.
- It's possible for your dream to come to pass.
- It's possible to step into the Promised Land.
- It's possible to have a blessed life, a rich life.

Just believe in God. All things are possible with God! All things are possible to the person who believes. If you want a better life, believe God. If you want a life of victory, believe God. If you want a life of power, believe God. All you have to do is just believe!

$

Chapter 14

Living above the Fray

Bad financial news is everywhere! With bank and corporate failures, stock market losses and a depressed housing market, rising unemployment, and inflation, money problems burden more and more of us. But do you realize that it's entirely possible even in this day and age, in this tough economy, in this depressed real estate market, and in this challenging job market to live above the fray—that is, to live in the glory of God and not be affected or tossed about by circumstances? "How can that be?" you may ask.

Well, think it about it. In the New Testament we see story after story of the apostles and how life changed after the day of Pentecost when the Holy Spirit fell on that upper room. From that time on nothing rattled the equilibrium of those anointed men.

That's because they were living in the glory, entirely secure in their identities as children of God and completely convinced that He would meet the need of the moment, whatever that happened to be. That scenario is best described by the sense that "I know that I know that I know," that it's a done deal because God said it and I believe it.

Take the apostle Peter for instance. In Acts 12 we see him consigned to prison, bound with chains between two guards who were assigned to keep him there until after the Passover, when he would be brought out before the people and no doubt executed. Despite the threat hanging over his head, he was so sound asleep that the angel of the Lord had to hit him in the side to wake him and set him free.

Right now you might be asking, "How could Peter have been sleeping so soundly, knowing he would soon be executed?" Because he knew . . .

that he knew . . . that he knew that God had everything under control. How could it have been otherwise? The church was fervently praying at that very moment.

Besides that, he had repeatedly witnessed God's glory displayed in any number of signs, wonders, miracles, healings, resurrections, and deliverances. Even his shadow contained the power to heal the sick. He was convinced beyond a shadow of a doubt that no matter what happened to him or around him, God could be glorified if he simply walked in faith and refused to let doubt or fear have any place inside him.

You and I have that same ability as we press on in true worship, making God's agenda our priority. If we make up our minds that whatever He says we will do and we do not veer from that plan, we can be at rest in the Holy Spirit, where all is well with nothing broken or missing. From that place we can be confident that we are pleasing God. That's how you as an individual can live above the fray in the very glory of God.

Perhaps you've struggled to believe God the way those anointed men did. Well, let me reassure you. It's never too late to walk out of timidity and doubt and into boldness, believing and declaring that Jesus is Lord over every situation you face.

To live above the fray is to not let the chaos surrounding you affect you. Although the world is in a recession and you live in the world, you do not think like the world because you are not of this world. More importantly your God is not in a recession. God has a purpose in the recession, but God is not in a recession.

By recession I don't have any sophisticated definition in mind. I just mean various financial setbacks like businesses slowing down, decreasing profits, massive layoffs, and joblessness, the bursting of the housing bubble, thousands of foreclosures, personal and business bankruptcies, bank failures, investment company collapses, the loss of retirement funds, and the social ills and unrest that go with the downturn. God is sovereign over these things. He foresees them all. He causes or permits them all, and when He causes or permits something, He does so with purpose and design. Here are a few Scriptures from the Bible to support God's purposes:

- "The lot is cast into the lap, but its every decision is from the Lord" (Proverbs 16:33).

- "Many are the plans in the mind of a man, but it is the purpose of the Lord that will stand" (Proverbs 19:21).
- "The Lord brings the counsel of the nations to nothing; he frustrates the plans of the peoples" (Psalm 33:10).
- "The Lord declares the end from the beginning . . . saying, 'My counsel shall stand, and I will accomplish all my purpose'" (Isaiah 46:10).

So none of the recessionary events has surprised the Lord. None of the events in your life has surprised God. His purposes and designs are being fulfilled according to plan.

One of my favorite Scriptures is Philippians 4:19. The promise from Philippians 4:19 is not contingent on what the government or the economy is doing or even our own ability. It is a promise from God, who is going to back up what He promised. God has promised to supply all your needs, and this promise is for today.

It is now and always has been God's intention to provide for his people. In Genesis 26:1 we see that there was a famine in the land and Isaac wanted to go down to Egypt to provide for his family, but God said, "Stay here, and I will be with you and will bless you. And I will perform the oath, which I swore unto Abraham your father" (Genesis 26:12). Then Isaac sowed in that land (during the famine) and received in the same year a hundredfold. And the Lord blessed him, and he became great (rich) and grew until he became very great. By this passage we understand that famines mean nothing to God, and He can and will bless you no matter what is going on with the economy if you will only be obedient.

You may look at your checkbooks, credit card statements, IRAs, or 401(k)s and get discouraged. But God isn't discouraged or even surprised at what is going on with your finances. Remember, Jesus said one of the main purposes for His being sent to earth was that we "might have life" and that we "might have it more abundantly" (John 10:10). The apostle John concurred, "Beloved, I wish above all things that thou mayest prosper and be in health" (3 John 2).

Prosperity is not a sin. It is a blessing. God is the greatest giver of abundance and prosperity. It is His will that we prosper and enjoy the good things in life. The bottom line is that God has given you all the tools you need to live above the fray.

$

Chapter 15

Remember When

Remember when God held you together when life was falling apart? Walk back through your memory and recount the times both small and great when He helped you rise up after circumstances tried to knock you down and keep you there. And don't forget that He even used the things that tried to bring you down to build you back up again. You were always on God's mind.

Because you were on His mind, He chose to promote you when others considered you unworthy. Because God was mindful of you, He brought you through every trial and trouble, foreclosure and failure, recession and ruin. Because He had you on His mind, He brought you through every kind of conflict and crisis.

It wasn't your winning personality, your impressive network of friends and colleagues, or your successful business endeavors that brought you this far without going under. It was no one but God and His great love for you.

Every imaginative and reflecting soul is moved and thrilled by the sight of the splendor of the hosts of heaven. David was no exception. When he lay on the Judean plains, watching and guarding his sheep, he was moved by the sublimity of the night. He was led to exclaim in the psalms, "When I consider thy heavens, the work of thy fingers, the moon and the stars which thou hast ordained; What is man, that thou art mindful of him? and the son of man that thou visitest him?"

It seemed wonderful to the psalmist that the exalted God who fills the heavens and whom the heaven of heavens cannot contain should waste a thought on such a creature as man. David recognized this concept. God has no concern for the stars, but He has the deepest concern over the fate of man. He never wept over burning suns, but He has wept over sinning and suffering man. He never expended any sympathy on the constellations, but the sorrows of men have awakened His deepest solicitude. He never visited a distant star to avert its fate or alter its doom, but He did visit this far, distant little planet to redeem man from destruction and visit him with the light and glory of a great salvation. He has proved to a certainty that He bestows more care and anxious love upon the humblest little babe in the poor man's cabin than upon all the material universe.

God has a marvelous and very peculiar interest in man. His relationship to His people is very special. In Psalm 8 people are crowned with glory and honor and made just a little lower than God. In the Genesis 1 story people are created in the image of God. And in all the creation stories . . . the rest of creation has been given as a gift for people.

No one cares more about your life than God. That's why He is paying careful attention to your life. What can possibly interest God in you? What can it possibly be about us? What can possibly even attract God's attention our way? What is it about man against the backdrop of space and against the generations of time? Why is God's mind full of us? Man must be something. He must occupy some role in the cosmos for God to stay connected to him.

God's love toward us is amazing. This is why He is never disconnected from what's going on and what's going down in your life. His is not sitting somewhere, distant and aloof, forcing you to face the music alone. Unlike human beings, He never turns away in disinterest. He doesn't have call waiting. He is never unreachable, unavailable, or too busy to notice your plight. No matter what's going on or where it takes place, it has not escaped His notice. And more than that, His attitude toward you is deeply compassionate. Scripture says that the Lord's tender mercies are new toward you every morning. Great is His faithfulness (Lamentations 3:23).

God sees you up close and personal. He sees your public self and the one that only you know. He is never unaware. Nor does He ignore the lob of even a single stone in your direction. He hears every lie others tell about you, every insult, and each piece of misdirection or sabotage aimed at your failure. He has seen every betrayal and bottled every tear. He sees your sleepless nights and knows every time someone backs you into a corner, when you can only wonder how you'll get through it in one piece. He sees it all and hears it all—every single injustice and every offense.

Interestingly enough, while He forgets your sins, He keeps track of each injustice, planning to right each wrong, turning around for good what the Enemy means for harm and restoring what was lost sevenfold. Isn't that the best news you've heard all day? It should make us dance a jig to know God loves us that much. Don't ever let yourself fall into the heresy that God is too busy or limited or indifferent to be concerned with you personally. You are on His radar all the time.

It's true that He responds unlike most humans. He wants to be involved. He wants to defend you. He never runs away from you in your struggles. And because you are faithful and refuse to give up when the chips are down, He says, "I am going to bless you. It doesn't matter that everyone else has counted you out, believing you are finished or defeated. I am going to bless you and pour out My favor upon you." So stop worrying and rejoice. Think about how He blessed you in the past. If I were you, I would get excited because God is getting ready to bless you big time.

$

Chapter 16

God is Searching Far and Wide

What on earth could God be searching for? I mean, it all belongs to Him! What could He possibly lack that He must look for? Scripture says He looks to and fro across the earth in search of those with faith.

Before we go any further, let me share a foundational truth that we must grasp in order to go on. First of all, Romans 8:1 tells us, "There is therefore now *no condemnation* to them that are in Christ Jesus, who walk not after the flesh but after the spirit." Why is there no more condemnation? Because once we've been saved, we are covered by the blood of Jesus, and God sees us as justified just as if we'd never sinned. Isn't that a stunning revelation? When God looks at us now, He simply sees us through the filter of the blood of Jesus, and He smiles at us, knowing the penalty for sin has been paid.

Why is that important? Because it means that we never have to fear God's wrath. We will never be required to pay for our own sin. It is finished, a dead issue. Praise God!

As a result we can take to the bank the Scripture in Matthew 9:22, which says, "Daughter (or son), be of good cheer. Your faith has made you whole. Go in peace." Another translation says it this way: "Daughter, cheer up. Your faith has made you well." The marvelous truth we see here is this: Everything is going to be all right because whatever we lack He is!

If the resurrection of Jesus truly did restore the blessings God intended for us—and we know it did—then we can stop grieving, weeping, complaining, striving, and sweating to earn God's love and blessing. We can stop begging God for what is already ours—health, provision, direction, the restoration of our love relationship with God and peace. The incredible news is that they're already ours, so all we have to do is take them!

Once we know those things are ours, we can simply rest, speaking in agreement with God, claiming our birthright as the children of God. That's why Psalm 107:2 tells us, "Let the redeemed of the Lord say so, whom he redeemed from the hand of the enemy." No matter what the situation all is well in the lives of believers because of Jesus, who turns every evil thing around for our good. That truth should bring us tremendous joy, knowing that in every area of our lives, He's got our backs and will make a way as we run to Him with our needs. Do you believe His grace is enough? Then get excited!

So how do we see ourselves from the moment we're saved? It can actually go in one of several directions. We can be so humble, so overwhelmed by His grace that we actually forfeit our inheritance because we never get off square one, or we can become proud because our status is no longer slaves but joint heirs with the King. Where is the balance?

Think of it this way. Many of us have such terrible opinions of ourselves that we are stunned with gratitude at the revelation of our marvelous redemption. Now before you misunderstand, let me make it clear that there's nothing wrong with gratitude. In fact, it's a very good thing. But what would happen if you, for example, won ten million dollars in the Publisher's Clearing House sweepstakes and sat at your kitchen table, weeping over the uncashed check for twenty years? What good would it be if it did nothing to change your life? In the same way we as believers must get past that stunned and grateful stage to rise up and move in the power that God has given us. Once we're saved, He wants us to act like generals taking orders from our supreme commander and moving out to do great exploits in Jesus' name. That's the only way this blessing is going to change the world for the kingdom of God.

On the other hand, we also need a healthy sense of humility.

Not long ago an evangelist told this story. His six-year-old son was squabbling with his four-year-old brother, and the two were really going at it. "I'm better than you." "No, I'm better than you." Finally in frustration the younger one said, "Why are you the best?"

The older one responded, "Because I'm a genius." Their dad frowned, knowing he had to deal with it, but at that moment he was unsure how to handle it.

After he prayed for several days, he sat down with his boys and explained, "You know, kids, the other day I heard you arguing about which of you was better than the other. And while I know I told you that nothing is impossible for you, I want you to know that it's not a good thing to boast. It's only because Jesus loves us that we can boast about anything. We want to love and serve Him because He first loved us. That's why from now on I want you to think about it this way: When someone asks you if you think you can do something amazing, you say, 'My daddy says I can." And if they ask, 'Who do you think you are that you can do that?' You say, 'My daddy says I can do all things because he is there to help me."

That's the kind of attitude we need, knowing that our confidence is not in our own goodness or talents but in God, who blesses us with everything we need to live out our destiny in the world. Once we've learned the balance that comes with knowing our identity in Christ, we can be confident that we are loved, equipped, and empowered by the Holy Spirit, who is the very God of glory Himself living inside us.

Now back to the subject, *God is Searching Far and Wide.* 2 Chronicles 16:9 says, *"For the eyes of the LORD run to and fro throughout the whole earth, to give strong support to those whose heart is blameless toward him."* What are we to understand by *the eyes of the Lord?* The Lord's eyes are upon all His people. He looks upon us not with loathing and contempt; but with commiseration which means consideration and compassion. He watches over us night and day to give us strong support or to show Himself strong in our lives. He shows himself strong by supplying our needs, whether spiritual or temporal; for he is *able to supply all of our needs, according to his riches in glory by Jesus Christ.*

"To run to and fro throughout the whole earth is expressive of his watchfulness over his people. God is diligent in His observation of us. He expresses himself in this very language in Jeremiah 31:28. He said, *"As I have watched over them, to pluck up, and to break down, and to throw down, and to destroy, and to afflict; so will I watch over them to build, and to plant, saith the Lord."*

God is searching for a righteous man to bless. He is searching the hearts of men and women everywhere. He is searching for a certain people to strengthen and demonstrate His might. Are you the one He's searching for?

$

Chapter 17

God is a Rewarder

I believe with all of my heart that God wants you to live a life of favor. I believe that God wants your life to be radically blessed coupled with favor and increase. I believe God wants you to prosper and be favor-conscious in everything you do. It's His promise to us in the Bible.

The Bible says God is a rewarder (Hebrews 11:6). The assertion that God is rewarding is the fact that God is so full and so completely self-sufficient that He overflows.

If we do not fully believe God is a rewarder for those who diligently seek Him, then we have very little purpose in prayer. As Christians, we must be persuaded that God delights in giving tokens of His goodness to His beloved children. This is a truth you must believe. You must believe it and receive it in your spirit that God loves to reward. Personally I love how God presented Himself to Abraham in the Bible. God said to Abraham that He (God) was his (Abraham's) exceedingly great reward (Genesis 15:1). Surely Abraham could have considered becoming the father of many nations a prize, but God said otherwise. Who needs rewards when you have God?

Receiving a reward is wonderful. It is recognition of something attained or accomplished. What is even more significant is the source of the reward. To receive a reward from the queen of England is greater than winning a carnival game. It is an honor to be invited to receive something from someone of great stature. Can you imagine what it is like to receive a reward from the Creator of all things! That is precisely what happens for those who seek Him. Hebrews 11:6 tells us that just to seek God results in a reward from God Himself. So seeking God must be a very special task for God to present a reward. And we would be foolish not to seek Him.

God is the rewarder, but He is also the reward for those who seek Him. The way we seek Him is through faith and belief "that He is" in all areas of life.

God is a recompenser, a remunerator—that is, a God who pays well for faithfulness. How does the Lord reward His diligent ones? It has been my experience that when I walk arm in arm with Jesus, His rewards break out on all sides in my life. Everything I do or have is blessed—my sons, friends, and ministry. There comes a life of Christ within that flows like a mighty river. Yes, we'll have trials and tribulations. But through it all He rewards us with manifestations of His presence.

God says we must believe He is a rewarder of faith. And He promised to reward our faith. The writer of Hebrews simply asserts that this is what faith does. Faith comes to God with the confidence that He is, and faith comes with the confidence that God will be a generous giver.

Let's talk about faith from the prospective of Hebrews 11:6. The faith that pleases God believes that God is. If you can't believe God created everything as He said, if you can't believe the Bible from the beginning, then you will not believe God in the other truths of faith. In other words, your faith must believe what God says. Faith does not say, "Show it to me, and I'll believe it." Faith says, "God said it. Therefore, I believe it—period!" Faith does not demand proof of purchase but trusts God.

The faith that pleases God also believes that He rewards those who diligently seek Him. There is a persistence to genuine faith. Abraham was promised that all the nations of the world would be blessed through him, but he died never seeing that promise. Did Abraham cease to believe just because he didn't see the fulfillment? Absolutely not! Genuine faith believes in God. It persists no matter what!

Notice that faith requires not only that we believe God exists but also that He is a rewarder of those who diligently seek Him. We are to seek Him, believing that it is in our best interest to do so, believing also that as we diligently seek Him, we receive something in return. So in this relationship of faith that we have with God, there is God interest, but that is also self-interest. And this self-interest is not merely incidental. It is required.

Throughout the stories of the Bible there are many evidences that God rewards those who seek Him. God rewarded the Old Testament priests with temporal provision for their service (Numbers 18:29-31). Boaz's praise and hope for Ruth demonstrated a deep belief that God would reward her for her faith and faithfulness to Naomi. He said, "The LORD repay you for what you have done, and a full reward be given you by the LORD, the God of Israel, under whose wings you have come to take refuge!" King David testified in Psalm 19:11 that "in keeping [God's law, testimony, precepts, and commandments] there is great reward."

God rewarded Ruth, the Moabite widow, when she believed the Lord and made Him her God (Ruth 1:16). The Bible tells us that she was given a "full reward" by the Lord when she came under His wings for refuge (Ruth 2:12). Not only did He give her protection, but He also gave her abundant provision, exceeding favor, and a glorious redemption (Ruth 2:9-17, 3:11, 4:10-13).

When Rahab, the harlot of Jericho, heard reports of how the Lord had opened up the Red Sea for the children of Israel, she believed that "He is God in heaven above and on earth beneath" (Joshua 2:9-11). Though Rahab had not personally witnessed the miracles, she *believed God* and hid the Jewish spies from their pursuers (Joshua 2:4-6). Because of her faith, she not only did not perish with those who did not believe (Joshua 6:25 and Hebrews 11:31) but was also given a place in the "hall of faith" in Hebrews 11.

God has promised blessings and benefits to those who seek Him, believe Him, trust in Him, listen to His voice, and walk in His ways. See, for example, Deuteronomy 28:1-14, where God promises wonderful blessing for those who "diligently obey" His voice and "observe carefully" His commandments (Deuteronomy 28:1).

Some will insist that we should not seek reward from God, that it somehow makes our faith and our motives impure. "Seek His face, not His hand," they say. But to follow that analogy, if you are like me, your hand is not far from your face, and the same is true of God. And the author of Hebrews teaches us something different. We must diligently seek God for who He is, but we must also believe that He rewards those who do so. Here are a few verses for meditation:

- Psalm 58:11 says, "Surely there is a **reward** for the righteous; surely there is a God who judges on earth."
- Proverbs 25:21-22 says, "If your enemy is hungry, give him bread to eat, and if he is thirsty, give him water to drink, for you will heap burning coals on his head, and the LORD will *reward* you."
- Isaiah 40:10-11 says, "Behold, the Lord GOD comes with might, and his arm rules for him; behold, his *reward* is with him, and his recompense before him."
- Isaiah 62:11 says, "Behold, the LORD has proclaimed to the end of the earth: Say to the daughter of Zion, 'Behold, your salvation comes; behold, his *reward* is with him, and his recompense before him.'"
- Matthew 5:11-12 says, "Blessed are you when others revile you and persecute you and utter all kinds of evil against you falsely on my account. Rejoice and be glad, for your *reward* is great in heaven, for so they persecuted the prophets who were before you."
- Hebrews 10:34-39 says, "Therefore do not throw away your confidence, which has a great *reward*. For you have need of endurance, so that when you have done the will of God you may receive what is promised."

We can talk about faith. We can study it. We can pray for it. But we have to exercise it if we want results from God. I am a witness that God will be faithful to His promises.

$

Chapter 18

Favor

This is a life-changing theme if we can get it deep into our spirits and live as if it is so.

How do you think God sees you? If you struggle to believe God loves you, it may be because you envision Him shaking His fist at you when you don't measure up. Perhaps that's the way you grew up, feeling inadequate, always wishing it were otherwise. Perhaps that's what your parents or other authority figures told you, but that's not how God sees you. He says He sees you through heaven's eyes, redeemed and made righteous by the blood of Jesus the moment you accepted His gift of salvation. He sees you with unlimited potential, and He has plans for you that are far greater than your wildest dreams.

If you feel inadequate as if God is down on you, you need to change the picture in your head and envision this instead: You're sitting, relaxing in a lawn chair alone in a peaceful meadow when Jesus walks toward you and smiles. He comes to where you're sitting, rests His hand gently on your head, and says He will bestow His favor upon you. If that picture doesn't strike a chord deep inside you, I don't know what will. Can you see it?

Whether or not you believe this scenario, it's true, so meditate on that and remind yourself that you are deeply favored by God more than you can even imagine. Tuck that truth deep in your spirit and bring it out any time the Devil accuses you or you feel tempted to accuse yourself or to wallow in perceived inadequacies or past failures. Those are merely lies of the Devil that can no longer victimize you unless you let them. In fact, the Devil was stripped of his dominion at the resurrection, so he can do absolutely nothing to you without your permission. So when he comes at you, tell him enough is enough, that from this moment on you are going to walk according to the truth of God's Word and refuse to believe anything that doesn't agree with it.

Psalm 5:12 says, "For you bless the righteous, O Lord; you cover him with favor as with a shield." And when you use your authority, you have the right to a spirit of favor around you in order to shield you. Remember when the twelve spies had the favor of God on them. They were protected when they entered the city where Rahab lived. Rahab had favor because she helped them. The bottom line is that when you are walking with God, you are encircled with His favor.

Before we go much favor in this discussion, we must define *favor.* Exactly what is favor? Favor is an action verb that is defined this way: "to impart supernatural favor" on your life. To favor means "to give special regard to, to treat with goodwill, to show exceptional kindness."

Favor means that God affords you advantages that will increase your success in every area of your life. The one who is favored is treated with a generosity far beyond what would normally be expected.

Favor means *grace*, which yields goodwill, benefit, and reward. It is something granted out of goodwill rather than for justice or payment.

Favor means to gain approval, acceptance, or special benefits from the Lord. Favor is having both heaven and the hand of God opened unto you.

The favor of God can mean that our requests are granted, that we are chosen for a position of honor, that we are looked kindly upon, that our enemies do not triumph over us, that others perceive us in a positive light, as good in their sights.

Favor can also be defined as a gift bestowed as a token of regard and preferential treatment. It can be described as the attainment of sudden blessings that we did not merit. It does not depend on how hardworking or resourceful an individual is. It is not a respecter of person, color, or race.

Favor is God's blessing on your life. Favor is God's kindness and benevolence, and it is given to those who love Him.

Favor is a gift from God. You didn't earn it. You can't buy it. You can't be so good that finally God will say, "You've been so good. You've earned favor."

Favor is the irresistible charisma of Christ that wraps itself around a person who has yielded him or herself to the fulfillment of the kingdom of God.

The favor of God is a twofold word. It is the attraction of God to you that releases influences through you so that other people are supernaturally inclined to like you, trust you, or cooperate with you. When people partner with you, they suddenly begin to experience the blessing of the Lord upon their lives, homes, or businesses.

My friend, you got mail. No, I'm sorry. You got favor. Favor is like resurrection power. It keeps raising you up no matter what tries to put you down. Favor is like a cork. When you put a cork under water, it pops right back up to the top. That's what favor does. It keeps you rising above every problem, every setback, and every situation in your life.

The favor of God is one of the most powerful things that can be released to you. And it is for the purpose of advancing the kingdom of God, not for the purpose of establishing your own kingdom.

$

Chapter 19

A Favor Only God Can Give

God, the eternal, self-existent being who created everything and sustains everything, is the source of our blessings. Every blessing comes out of Him to us. We are only a temporary trustee. Everything we own, everything we have comes from God. No matter how much money we get or how many things we collect, it comes from God, and it belongs to God. It is not ours. It's His. We are just holding God's wealth for Him, using what we need of it to live on. So whether it's money, land, or possessions, we will never be rightly related to what we have until we recognize that it is not ours. Again all that we have belongs to God. All things are from Him and through Him. Whatever we have originates from the LORD.

Your first thought may be that what you have belongs to you. Wrong. It belongs to God. Why? God owns everything. Everything in the ground, everything above the ground, everything in the air, everything that passes through the air belongs to God. He owns the cattle on a thousand hills, the wealth in every mine. First Chronicles 29:11 reads, "For all that is in heaven and in earth is Yours." Scripture also inform us, "The earth is the Lord's and the fullness thereof" (Psalm 24:1). So what belongs to God? The earth and everything in it! Whatever we have, it belongs to God. When we grasp this fact, we will begin to understand that anything He made is His property and He shares His property with us. Do you realize that God, the Creator of all things, including the air you breathe, claims ownership of all that exists? Understanding this important biblical principle is in fact the first key to financial success!

In Exodus 19:5 God Almighty says, "All the earth is mine." Through Moses's inspired pen we read, "Behold, the heaven and the heaven of heavens is the Lord's thy God, the earth also, with all that therein is" (Deuteronomy 10:14). "For every beast of the forest is mine, and the cattle upon a thousand hills . . . . The world is mine, and the fullness thereof," claims our Maker (Psalm 50:10, 12). According to the Bible, *your* money and *your* income rightfully belongs to God. "The silver is mine, and the gold is mine, saith the Lord of hosts" (Haggai 2:8).

I believe these Scriptures are written in the Bible because God wants us to view what we have (whether it is much or little) with the right perspective. And the right perspective is that our possessions are gifts from Him. God is the great giver or provider of every good and perfect gift. The apostle James calls our attention to God being the great giver of gifts when he wrote, "Every good gift and every perfect gift is from above, and cometh down from the Father of lights, with whom is no variableness, neither shadow of turning" (James 1:17). "Good gift" speaks of the act of giving and confirms once again that God is a giving God. "Perfect gift" refers to the object of the gift. Perfect also means there is nothing evil or bad that comes from God. James points out very clearly that God is the source of everything good and God's good gifts are also perfect. We can be assured that God always wills the best for His children.

I am so happy that God sends good and perfect gifts from heaven down to us. Three of those gifts are favor, blessings, and increase.

When God's favor is poured out on someone, it makes a world of difference in his or her life. If you have lived much life at all, you are probably well aware that putting your trust in the economy, your employer, or your bank account is not a good idea. They are all fair-weather friends. They can all help you greatly one minute, and then the next everything has changed. But when you have God's favor, there is nothing in life that can hold you down or hold you back. Favor will release great blessings, including prosperity, health, opportunity, and advancement in your life. We find this to be true in the life of Joseph.

In the Bible Potiphar's wife slandered Joseph and lied about him. As a result, he was thrown in prison. Yet in prison Joseph had supernatural favor that caused him to be put in charge of all of the inmates. When Joseph interpreted Pharaoh's dream, he was promoted and set over all the land of Egypt (Genesis 41:39-41). Joseph walked in favor with God. He was elevated to a place of favor because of his faithfulness. Wherever Joseph went, God's favor was with him.

Abram left his father's house and followed God, not knowing where he would go (Genesis 12:1-3). He was later called Abraham, and he believed God fully and obtained the promised son (Isaac). Abraham was visited by God in Genesis 18:1-3,

> And the Lord Yahweh appeared to him in the plains of Mamre, and he sat in the tent door in the heat of the day. And he lift up his eyes and looked, and, lo, three men stood by him, and when he saw them, he ran to meet them from the tent door, and bowed himself toward the ground. And said, my Lord, if now I have found favor in your sight, pass not away, I pray you, from your servant.

David was called a man after God's own heart, and he walked in the favor of God. King Saul tried many times to kill David, but God's favor covered him. David writes in Psalm 20:1-2 and 5-8,

> I will extol You, O Lord Yahweh; for You have lifted me up, and have not made my foes to rejoice over me. O Lord Yahweh my God, I cried to You and You have healed me. For His anger endures but for a moment; in His favor is life; weeping may endure for a night, but joy comes in the morning. And in my prosperity I said, I shall never be moved. Lord Yahweh, by Your favor You have made my mountain to stand strong; you did hid Your face, and I was troubled. I cried to You, O Lord Yahweh; and to the Lord Yahweh, I made supplication.

Daniel walked in the favor of God. Daniel was one of the children of Israel who had been taken to Babylon, and Daniel was determined in his heart not to defile himself with the king's food. Daniel 1:9 says, "Now God had brought Daniel into favor and tender love with the prince of the eunuchs." Daniel requested to be tested ten days on vegetables and water, and the prince of the eunuchs agreed. Daniel was cast into the den of lions, but he was not harmed. He told the king, "My God has sent His angel, and has shut the lions' mouths, that they have not hurt me; forasmuch as before Him innocency was found in me; and also before you, O king, have I done no hurt" (Daniel 6:22).

Favor kept Joseph, Abram, David, and Daniel afloat in difficult and challenging times because they were walking in God's favor, which is walking in God's blessing.

The favor of God rests on a certain nation or person. And it has purpose. Who obtains favor from the Lord? You! Once you receive Jesus Christ, you become a favored person. "For whoever finds me finds life, and obtains favor from the Lord" (Proverbs 8:35).

When you have God's favor, you are fully empowered to succeed. Tap into God's favor. Set your atmosphere for favor. The favor of God will charge your circumstances. It will open doors for you, make ways for you, and bring tremendous increase in your life.

When the Lord gave me the sermon *FBI* in 1998, my position at a well-known company had just been eliminated. From a cash standpoint I was flat broke—so broke that I had to apply for welfare. I had thousands of expenses on my personal credit cards, accumulating interest at a very high rate. I had no home to refinance because I was renting. In addition, I had two small children who were looking to me to provide for their needs because I was separated from my husband *(now deceased)*. I had no job, no money, and no savings.

In the middle of this situation the Lord spoke three words to me—favor, blessing, and increase. He spoke these words to me while I was reading Psalm 115:12-15,

> The LORD hath been mindful of us: he will bless us; he will bless the house of Israel; he will bless the house of Aaron. He will bless them that fear the LORD, both small and great. The LORD shall increase you more and more, you and your children. Ye are blessed of the LORD which made heaven and earth.

These Scriptures knocked me to the floor in prayer. They literally took my breath away. I could hardly believe that it was actually saying what it was saying! When I ended my prayer, I read the Scriptures again like this:

> The LORD hath been mindful of Barbara: he will bless Barbara; he will bless the house of Barbara. He will bless Barbara because she fears the LORD. The LORD shall increase Barbara more and more, Barbara and her children. Barbara is blessed of the LORD which made heaven and earth.

As I declared this word over and over again, there was an excitement that rose up inside me. This was God telling me that He promised to bless and prosper me. No longer did I declare I was broke. I begin to declare that I was walking in favor, blessing, and increase.

I was approved for welfare, and I faithfully paid my tithes to the church. I can testify that I never missed a rent payment or any other payment. My sons never missed a meal, and I never had to borrow money from anyone. After I received welfare for eight months (the number of completion), amazingly God opened a door for me to purchase my first home with no job. Literally! I had no full-time or permanent employment. God gave me favor with the broker, the realtor, and the bank. In the meantime I was preaching the sermon *FBI* to everyone. I preached the sermon until *FBI* became a reality in my life. Through this process I learned that the when the favor of God is on you, opportunities will come your way—opportunities for blessings and increase.

Was it easy? No, but I kept believing God's Word. Soon I had just enough. But God didn't stop there. He shifted me from just enough to more than enough. God began to pour out an outflowing of financial blessings in my life.

If you are in a desperate situation, I invite you to tap into the favor of God by believing God's Word. The Word of God is living, active, and full of power. Meditate on the Scriptures related to favor. Put them on your refrigerator, bathroom mirror, or your desk. Then begin to prophesy it over your life, your children, your church, and your nation. Why? God wants to pour out His favor on you individually, on us corporately, and on your children. He wants you to live a much more fulfilled life. I found out that the favor of God will produce and cause the following:

- Supernatural increase and promotion (Genesis 39:21)
- Restoration of everything that the Enemy has stolen from me (Exodus 3:21)

- Honor in the midst of adversaries (Exodus 11:3)
- Increased assets, especially in the area of real estate (Deuteronomy 33:23)
- Great victories in the midst of great impossibilities (Joshua 11:20)
- Recognition even when it seems unlikely I'll receive it (1 Samuel 16:22)
- Prominence and preferential treatment (Esther 5:8)
- Policies, rules, regulations, and laws changed and reversed to my advantage (Esther 8:5)
- Won battles I won't even have to fight because God will fight them for me (Psalm 44:3)

The more you begin to speak out about God's favor, the more you will begin to experience it in your life. So make it a choice today to believe that God's favor, miracles, and blessings will unfold before you this day!

$

Chapter 20

The Year of God's Favor

Too often we see wealth in terms of having an abundance of material or worldly things. Riches consist of how many cars you own or how many square feet are in your house. But favor is a lot more than money. The fact is when you have favor, you don't need money. When you have God's favor, there is nothing in life that can hold you down or hold you back. The favor of God will change what men say is impossible. It will bring you success. Favor will break through any barriers set before you.

I strongly believe this is the year of the Lord's favor! So what exactly does that mean for you? How can you step into this reality and experience God's favor in your life, your job, your relationships, and your money.

In Isaiah 61 favor is initiated with proclamation! Favor is not passive. Favor is the anointing of the Holy Spirit to proclaim and release healing, deliverance, blessing, and prosperity. The Message Bible translates it this way: "This is God's year to act!" In the year of God's favor impossible situations turn around. In the year of God's favor chains that once held you back are loosened. In the year of God's favor the atmosphere is pregnant with miracles, signs, and wonders. In the year of favor waste places are restored, missed opportunities redeemed, and dreams reawakened.

So when the Bible declares that the Lord will bless "the righteous" with favor in Psalm 5:12, it means you and me! In *Webster's Dictionary* the definition of favor includes "friendly or kind regard; good will; approval; liking; unfair partiality; favoritism; attractiveness; to be partial to; prefer; to help; assist; to do a kindness for; endorsing; specially privileged." Just think about that! God wants to give you special privileges. That is why in the midst of a world that seems increasingly dark and difficult, the Bible tells us that from God's perspective we are living in an extremely favorable time.

You may feel barren, desolate, unproductive, useless, and insignificant. But now is the time to get the revelation and understand that this year is the year of the favor of the LORD. It is the year of breaking forth, breaking through, and breaking out. It is the time of your expansion, the enlargement of your territory, the increase of your resources and your influence. It is the season of fruitfulness and fulfillment and the habitation of God's glory in your life.

Every time favor is mentioned in the Holy Scripture, it is accompanied by a specific picture of what favor looks like. Isaiah 61 tells us what to expect in the year of God's favor—an increase in His presence and anointing; healing, deliverance, salvation, restoration, promotion, increase, joy! Israel experienced God's favor, and her enemies showered her with silver and gold. Joseph walked in favor, and he was promoted from the lowest dungeon to the palace. Esther experienced favor, and the unchangeable laws of the Medes and the Persians were reversed to bring deliverance to her entire nation.

We all need to become favor-minded! We must become conscious of God s desire to bestow His divine favor upon us. In other words, we need to consciously and daily declare and affirm the favor of God upon our lives. The more that we declare that "this is the year of the Lord's favor in my life," the more we will experience it. We all need to change our thinking and begin to speak our new mind-set as follows:

- God's favor goes before me.
- God's favor opens doors for me that no man can shut.
- God's favor overtakes me wherever I go.

The Scripture teaches that the time of the church's favor has come. The Bible says, "Thou shalt arise, and have mercy upon Zion: for the time to favour *her* yea, the set time, is come!" (Psalm 102:13). The *her* is the church.

Let us recognize the favor of God as identified in a few Old Testament passages.

- But Noah found *grace* (graciousness, kindness, favor) in the eyes of the LORD (Genesis 6:8).
- And Joseph found *grace* (graciousness, kindness, favor) in his sight, and he served him: and he made him overseer over his house (Genesis 39:4).
- Gideon told God, "If now I have found *grace* (graciousness, kindness, favor) in thy sight, then shew me a sign that thou talkest with me" (Judges 6:17).
- Ruth said, "Then she said, Let me find *favour* (graciousness, kindness, favor) in thy sight, my lord" (Ruth 2:13).
- And the child Samuel grew on, and was in *favour* (graciousness, kindness, favor) both with the LORD, and also with men (1 Samuel 2:26).
- Saul sent to Jesse, saying, "Let David, I pray thee, stand before me; for he hath found *favour* (graciousness, kindness, favor)in my sight" (1 Sam 16:22).

God's supernatural favor flowing in your life is not based on your background, looks, or personality. His favor is based on the Word of God and believing what it says about you. Understand that if God has promised you favor, your present circumstances do not dictate your future conditions because God has spoken His Word and it is a good word.

I strongly believe when you activate your faith for God's favor, it will work for you. Someone may not particularly like you or your personality, but that doesn't matter. You believe in God's ability to influence them, and He will. I have discovered that the favor of God will cause people to go out of their way to bless you without even knowing why they're doing it.

Let us prepare ourselves and praise God to maximize God's favor in our lives. This is the year of God's favor. God is ready to release favor, blessing, and increase over you. Get ready to receive them.

$

Chapter 21

When You Have God's Favor

When you have His favor, He shows His partiality toward you. Walking in God's favor is to walk in His blessings. And it is my prayer that God's favor rests upon you all the days of your life.

The Bible records numerous examples of God's favor upon His people. One example is Joseph. Joseph experienced God's favor and went from prison to the palace. The widow who offered her last meal of grain to the man of God did not in return find her pantries overflowing with substance but instead had supernatural access to daily provision.

It is not God's way of lording one person over another or lavishly blessing one of His children while His other children look on in want and need. Although favor can bring pleasure, it serves a greater purpose when it truly comes from God. Favor is a spiritual advantage for the purposes of expanding His kingdom, not for building yours. Believing God exists isn't the same as trusting the God who exists.

While studying the Bible, I have realized that its pages are filled with men and women who have operated under the manifest favor of God to accomplish great feats to advance His kingdom. In the overwhelming majority of these events the favor of God was not displayed as excess provision as much as it was supernatural intervention in the deficiency of provision.

Which of the following do you think is greater: Wealth in the hands of the foolish or a little in the hands of the wise? Realize that God does not have to saturate you with excess resources just to get a job done or to make others see you as a success. God's greatest demonstration of power does not occur when He operates within the world's views and standards but when He defies them altogether.

David had God's favor. In Psalm 23:6 he said "Surely goodness and mercy will follow me all the days of my life." David was saying, "Favor follows me everywhere I go." David knew he had a Christian advantage of God's favor. He knew he could expect preferential treatment. He knew God would assist him. David had a mentality of God's favor. Have you ever read the book of Psalms? All through Psalms David constantly talks about God's favor, and you should talk about it as well.

My friend, God wants to pour out His goodness and grace upon you. He wants to help you get ahead in this life. He wants to lead you to the right decision. He wants to lead you to the right job. He wants to lead you to the right relationship. God truly wants to do more for you than you can possibly ask or even think. Ephesians tells us that He wants to show us the immeasurable, limitless, surpassing greatness of His free favor. In other words, God wants to go far and above what we're used to! He truly wants to show you favor in unusual and extraordinary ways. This is His gift to each of us.

So start setting your hopes higher today and increase your expectations of what God's favor will do in your life. Pray to Him for His unlimited favor, and you will start to experience the abundance He has in store for you!

When it comes to God's favor and His grace and blessings, it has nothing to do with earning it. It has nothing to do with being worthy of it. His grace and favor have been extended to us regardless of our response. He is the one who made the promises. He is the one who will keep His Word. He is the one who has extended Himself to us. No, you cannot earn His favor. Neither can I. No, you do not deserve His favor. Neither do I. But it has been extended to us. Anticipate, look for, and expect God's favor in your life.

When you have God's favor, He will give you the land. He will shut every door that needs to be closed and open doors that are shut. He will give you the opportunity to succeed.

When you have God's favor, the following occurs:

- It brings success your way.
- It makes your crooked places straight.

- It causes people to help you.
- It will take you places you couldn't go on your own.
- It leads to favor with man.
- Blessings will chase you down.
- Good things will happen on your behalf.
- Difficulties and challenges turn into blessing for you.
- Your territory will be enlarged.
- Doors of opportunities will open.
- Your enemies will not triumph over you.
- You will live in houses you did not build.
- You will receive venues you did not grow.
- You'll walk in promotion!
- You'll experience increase!

If you choose to have a favor mentality today, you can enjoy the goodness and mercy that God has stored up for you!

You will notice in this book that I frequently quote the Holy Scripture. I do so because God promises that His Word "will not return to me empty, but will accomplish what I desire and achieve the purpose for which I sent it" (Isaiah 55:11). God never makes this promise about my words or yours. As you continue reading this book, let the truth of God's Word validate your thinking.

$

Chapter 22

Blessings!

God promised to bless you. To begin with, the blessing of God doesn't consist of things. The blessing of God will produce things, but the blessing isn't things. Galatians 3:14 says, "That the blessing of Abraham might come on the Gentiles through Jesus Christ; that we might receive the promise of the Spirit through faith." Abraham's blessing has come upon us through faith in Christ, and the blessing isn't the things that Abraham possesses. Would you want Abraham's animals that have been dead for four thousand years? Do you want his tents and clothes? I don't think so. What you want is the favor of God that was spoken over Abraham. God's favor will produced physical and spiritual abundance in your life right now.

The good news is that you are already blessed. The bad news is that most don't know the power of that blessing. So let's first deal with the words *blessed* and *blessing*. If you are *blessed*, it means you are personally and especially favored by God. The word *blessing* is an action verb that is defined this way: "to impart supernatural favor" on your life. The word *blessing* is defined as the empowerment to be successful. It is God imparting a supernatural enabling into your life. It means to walk in God's abundant harvest with an uncanny ability to succeed and triumph over adversity.

Ephesians 1:3 is the only Scripture verse in the New Testament of the Bible where the word *blessings* is used. The Scripture reads, "Blessed be the God and Father of our Lord Jesus Christ, who hath blessed us with all spiritual blessings in heavenly places in Christ." We do not have to ask for this blessing because He has already blessed us with every spiritual blessing in the heavenly places in Christ! God is the source of all spiritual blessings. Christ is the great blessing from God. And we are the recipients of these blessings because we are in Christ. God chose to bless us in Christ according to His nature and will.

Though we may have been taught otherwise, there is absolutely nothing wrong with asking God to bless us. After all, He is our Jehovah Jaireh and actually calls Himself by that name in His Word. From the moment of creation He planned to provide for His people. He doesn't want us to go elsewhere for blessing. He expects us to go to Him, the source of all blessing. In fact, it is God's very nature to bless His children. It is not only His prerogative but His great delight to bless us—far more than a loving human parent ever could. We know how much we delight in blessing our children, don't we?

Throughout the ages Christians have desired the blessings of the Lord. In the Old Testament we see Jacob being so desirous of the covenant blessing that he was willing to deceive his father, Isaac, in order to obtain it.

As Christians, we want God to bless our ministry, our plans, our church, our sermons, our families, our homes, our jobs, our businesses, our tithes and offerings, etc. Why do we desire them? We know that without God's blessing there will not be a greater ministry, more miracles, greater prosperity, and better health and success in all our endeavors! So we ask God to bless our efforts in the work that we do for Him as well as for the things that please us.

But have you ever wondered whether your definition of God's blessing matches God's definition? Do God's blessings always lead to what we call success? Despite the fact that we use the word *blessing* or *bless* lavishly in our prayers and in our speech, do we only have a vague idea of its true meaning? We know it means something good, but do we know what good is?

As we researched its meaning, we were rather surprised to find that one of the Greek words from which our English word *blessing* is translated is *eulogia*. It is made up of two Greek words, namely *eu*, meaning good or well, and *logos*, meaning word. It means "to bless or speak well of." The Greek word *eulogia* refers to one upon whom God has acted or who has experienced His blessing. *Eulogeso* means the following: "I have done this for you and I will do it for the nations through you as well."

In Psalm 103:1-2 we are told to bless the Lord. "Bless the Lord, O my soul, and all that is within me, bless His holy name. Bless the Lord,

O my soul, and forget none of His benefits." How can we bless the Lord? How can we bless Him who has everything? Although He is not in need of anything, it's so exciting to see that we can bless Him by praising Him and speaking well of Him! It blesses God when our hearts are completely filled with thanksgiving toward Him for all the benefits He bestows on us! God is not in need of praise, but it pleases Him when we speak truth! We need to realize that God is the source of our blessings!

We have a wonderful promise in Galatians 3:8-9, "The Scripture, foreseeing that God would justify the Gentiles by faith, preached the gospel beforehand to Abraham, saying, 'All the nations will be blessed in you . . . So then those who are of faith are blessed with Abraham, the believer.'" As we walk by faith, we are blessed together with Abraham!

At this point I'd like to dig deeper into the names of God. In the Old Testament Scriptures written in the original Hebrew, the names of God describe His character like the one we just looked at—Jehovah Jaireh, meaning provider, which is also translated to "the Lord will provide."

The other names include but are not limited to following:

- **El Raffa**—our healer; the Lord who heals.
- **El Elohiym**—the God of all power and majesty.
- **El Shalom**—the God of peace and all well-being who completes us so that nothing is broken or missing.
- **El Nissi**—our protector, banner or rallying point, and means of our victory in battle.
- **El Rayah**—our Shepherd, the one who cares and is fully committed to the well-being of His sheep.
- **El Shaddai**—the all-sufficient one who supplies our deepest longings; also translates as the "all-breasted one."
- **El Shama**—the Lord who is here; His presence that never leaves.
- **El Adonai**—the Lord God, who, because of His greatness, is worthy of all our praise; supreme Lord of all.
- **El Tsitkinu**—our righteousness; it is by Him that we are made righteous.
- **El Eliown**—the supreme, the Most High; implies strength, sovereignty, and supremacy.

When we combine the character traits in all the names of God, we see that there is no need that He does not supply for. We can count on that reality, knowing that He designed us to share intimacy with Him and has all our bases covered.

It is God's desire to bless and prosper you and to give you favor. He wants to bless you and prosper all that you do. And He wants to bless you today. After all, He sent His beloved Son to the earth and raised Him to be seated at His right hand for that very purpose. So hear him saying to you what He said to Abraham, "I will bless you."

Because you belong to Him, you have a right to be more blessed than everybody else. God wants to bless you wherever you go—in the city and in the field, your arrival and your leaving. Moreover, God wants you blessed in all things—your body, your bank account, your job, your business, and your land. He wants you abundantly prosperous.

Have you ever been run down by a blessing? I guarantee you that after a blessing runs you down, you will get back up and say, "Hit me again." God, our provider and Jehovah Jireh, is eager to run you over with blessings. He is eager to pour His blessing out over you. The Lord, who made heaven and earth, has always been pleased to bless His people. And it's time to break forth into the prosperity that God had destined for you.

I sense that many of you reading this are saying, "Now is the time to be blessed!" You are ready to prosper in new ways and to see multiplication in your life. You are ready for your next season to be filled with prosperity and for every seed you've sown to bring many treasures back to you. Well, I'm writing to tell you that God is ready to release blessing and prosperity over you. It is His desire to give it to you. Now get ready to receive them.

God is a rewarder (Hebrews 11:6). In fact, He loves to reward. He says to us, "I am your shield, your exceedingly great reward" (Genesis 15:1). We are also told, "The righteous will be rewarded in the earth" (Proverbs 11:31), not just in heaven but down here on earth. These Scriptures confirm that God's desire is to reward you with His blessings now.

God has a blessing belonging to a particular people. The Bible says, "You are blessed by the Lord." Who are these distinguished people? They are a people whom God has blessed because He willed to do so. The will of God alone is the source of the rich, eternal, saving blessing, which abounds toward the Lord's elect. If you are blessed by the Lord, who made heaven and earth, you have His favor.

I love God's blessings. Why? "The blessings of the Lord make one rich, and he adds no sorrow with it" (Proverbs 10:22). The word *sorrow* is translated as *toil.* Toil means struggle, battle, laborious, and effort. So what is God saying to us in the Scripture? The blessing will cancel out toiling for a living. In other words, you do not have to labor continuously, work hard, or struggle strenuously for the blessings. God simply drops the blessing on your life. You do not have to toil in exchange for the blessing of God. The blessing from God will work on your behalf.

The Word of God says, "The blessing makes—" The word *make* means to "to cause to happen to" or "to cause to occur or appear." God brings the blessing to you. And there is power in the blessing to make you rich. I believe the most desirable kind of wealth is not just having abundance but having it with no sorrow mixed in. This Scripture confirms that the Lord's blessing is our greatest wealth.

Let's reexamine the word *bless.* The word *bless* includes words such as *blessed* and *blessing.* In general, the word *bless* means happy, fortunate, prosperous, or the act of wishing good for someone. The Hebrew *barak* (to bless) means to empower, to enable to succeed, prosper, be fertile, live long, etc. It is the bestowal or conferral of abundant and effective life on someone or even something. I also discovered that a blessing is an act of declaring or wishing God's favor and goodness upon others. A blessing involves not only the good effect of the words, but when it's inspired by the Holy Spirit, a blessing also has the power to bring those words of favor to pass in your life.

A blessing starts with words. It is real. It is tangible, and it even carries visible substance. Therefore, blessings are not merely words spoken. Rather, blessings include the power to bring about that declaration. There are two different emphases of the word *bless* used in the Old Testament and the New Testament.

The word *bless* in the Old Testament is derived from a Hebrew word that literally meant "to kneel." This was a sign of adoration (see Psalms 103:1 and 2; 145:1 and 2). The word *bless* in the Old Testament was used mostly as a verb, which means that it referred to an activity or gesture. There are at least three modes of blessings.

1. God blesses us (Genesis 1:22 and 28; Acts 3:25-26).
2. We bless God (Deuteronomy 8:10).
3. We bless others (Genesis 49:1-28).

God blesses us by giving us gifts both temporal and spiritual. We consider such gifts as a blessing from God because of His mercy and grace and not because we earned it. We bless God when we show our gratitude for what He has done for us (His blessings). We bless others by declaring or wishing God's favor and goodness upon others.

The New Testament's emphasis on the concept of blessing is on the fact of being blessed. Whereas the Old Testament speaks much about *blessing* or *bless*, the New Testament speaks much about being blessed. The Beatitudes is an excellent example of this concept (Matthew 5:3-12). The fundamental concept of blessing in the New Testament is that we are already blessed. Blessings do not come from riches and possessions. Blessings ultimately come because of what God has done. We are already blessed because of the fact that we are part of the body of Christ.

We don't serve God or obey God to receive His blessing or great wealth. That would not produce blessings from God because of the improper motives of serving God. We obey God because we love God and we trust Him. And God's love (blessing) will overtake us, and we won't have to worry about what we shall eat or drink or what we will put on today. We will walk in the confidence that God, our heavenly Father, will take care of us.

Deuteronomy 8:10 says, "When you have eaten and are full, then you shall bless the LORD your God for the good land which He has given you."

The word *bless* in this verse means to thank God and to show adoration for His mercy and grace upon you. Basically we have to give God His dues. Otherwise the temptation of pride might begin to grow and prosper. So the question is this: What do you do when you experience the blessing of God? Do you thank Him and recognize that what you received was not because of your own work? We should be careful to bless God when we experience and enjoy God's blessing. When you obtain a new home, car, job, or business contract, remember God. All things belong to God, and ultimately He prospers you. Don't think for a moment that the things you have are solely due to your own efforts and smarts. Remember that God has blessed you. Therefore, you should honor God and bless Him.

$

Chapter 23

Blessings: The Result of God's Favor

In the Bible a blessing is depicted as a mark of God's relationship with a person or nation. When a person or group is blessed, it is a sign of God's grace upon them and presence among them.

When God puts a promise in our heart, He will always give us some kind of sign to confirm His Word that the promise is going to come to pass. It may be a confirmation through a dream, a person, nature, or even something that seems like a coincidence. It may look insignificant to others, but to you it will resonate in your spirit, reminding you that God is in control and directing your steps.

Christians were created for blessings. After God created mankind, He made a decree. "God blessed them" (Genesis 1:28). As stated earlier in this book, the word *bless* means "to confirm prosperity of happiness upon." Blessings speak of the goodness of God. Imagine for a moment your life being full of everything good all the time. That is what it means to be blessed!

The favor of God will change every negative aspect of your life. Like the laws of gravity, there are favor laws that operate in the universe. When we consciously declare God's favor in our lives, we abundantly receive blessings.

Let me ask the question, "Are you living under the same faith as that of Abraham?" If you claim that you live in the same faith as Abraham, then you should be able to proclaim that you are blessed with faithful Abraham (Gal 3:9). Notice how Paul described the promises of God toward Abraham and the inclusion of those promises to the gentiles, That the blessing of Abraham might come on the Gentiles through Jesus Christ; that we might receive the promise of the Spirit through faith (Galatians 3:14). He continues, "Now to Abraham and his seed were the promises made" (Galatians 3:16).

Paul taught that the seed (singular) was a direct reference to Jesus, the Messiah. However, Paul made reference to much more than the Messiah's association with the promises of Abraham. He also wrote, "If ye be Christ's, then are ye Abraham's seed, and heirs according to the promise" (Galatians 3:29). You are heirs according to the promise! If we belong to Christ—that is to say, if He is the Lord of our life—then we are heirs according to the promise. Whatever God promised Abraham, He has also promised to the normal everyday Christian! Abraham's blessings are yours too!

If you are Abraham's seed, then blessings are already directed your way. Blessings will come upon you and overtake you. Why don't you take a moment and declare (release) the favor of God on your life by repeating these affirmations:

- I am a child of the King, and His favor is on my life!
- The favor of God goes before me and produces success in my life!
- The favor of God will manifest itself in my life today!
- The favor of God is on my life, and the Enemy will never triumph over me.
- Because of God's favor, I will never be defeated!
- Because I have God's favor, I am blessed and will walk daily in supernatural blessings.

God's favor on your life is supernatural. In other words, it supersedes natural circumstances. The favor of God is the difference between winning and losing, between success and failure! His favor yields blessings and rapid promotion. Thing will begin to work together for your good without any effort of your own.

Did you know that one aspect of the favor of God is designed to set His people apart as a distinct nation? We are to be a people whose priorities, morality, and culture stand out against the backdrop of our surrounding culture (Deuteronomy 4:6-8). God gave the Law so that His people could experience the mystery of divine love (Leviticus 18:1-5 and Matthew 22:34-40). Idolatry and immorality might be fine for the pagan nations, but Israel was to be a people holy to the Lord. They were to stand out by the fervor with which they loved the Lord and by the diligence with which they loved one another. The Law of God unfolded His plan for Israel's sanctification. Sadly the people of God in the Old Testament never quite seemed to understand this aspect of God's favor.

And we're not much different from the Israelites. When considering moral issues or personal decisions, we love to ask, "What would Jesus do?" That's easy. He would keep the Law of God. He fulfilled all the priestly regulations, the sacrifices that took place in the tabernacle and temple, and replaced them with sacraments of His own (baptism, the Lord's Supper, etc.). He also fulfilled the Ten Commandments and the principles of equity embedded in the civil code of Israel. Now He expects us to follow His example and pursue holiness in the Lord (2 Corinthians 7:1). We must live within the parameters of the Law, a law that now incorporates liberty and love (Romans 7.12).

Too many followers of Christ are content to slurp at the drippings of God's favor rather than drink from the fire hose. We need to recognize that there is no favor with God unless we have *all* the favor of God.

You are invited to live in the blessings of God. God wants to open the doors of favor to you. How do you enter? Let's begin by looking at a few bible characters that experienced favor, so we can define this year by what God is saying and begin to prophetically proclaim it.

Samuel had God's Favor

The Bible says, "And the child Samuel grew on, and was in favor both with the LORD, and also with men" (1 Samuel 2: 26). Samuel as a child had a difficult time in that he was away from his family and friends. Maybe Samuel lived a life of solitude early on in his life. Eli the priest, his possible mentor, was not a very good example to follow. Eli's sons could have been a very bad influence on the child. Yet when children are safe under God's favor, it is a shield around them from all wrong and negative influences. When Samuel was of age, he had a very big role in Israel. He was the only person in the history of Israel who was in the office of a prophet, a priest, and a judge.

Favor can protect from everything till the divine destiny is unfolded.

Esther had God's Favor

"And Esther obtained favor in the sight of all them that looked upon her" (Esther 2:15). Esther pleased the king and won his favor. Immediately he provided her with her beauty treatments and special food. He assigned to her seven maids selected from the king's palace and moved her and her maids into the best place in the harem. Sometimes it is not the confident personality that brings in the success. It is a need for the favor of God to flood our lives. We need to practice brokenness. Esther finally turned out to be the queen of the vast empire, as God's favor was upon her.

Daniel had God's Favor

Now God had brought Daniel into favor and tender love with the prince of the eunuchs (Daniel 1:9). Like all the champions in the Bible mentioned above, Daniel, too, was broken. Away from home friends and parents, his heart was perhaps lonely. He, too, did not compromise on principles of God. He kept himself holy in his food habits and morality. God promoted him as the prime minister of the vast empire where he once was a captive.

Israelites received God's Favor

"And I will give this people favor in the sight of the Egyptians: and it shall come to pass, that, when ye go, ye shall not go empty" (Exodus 3: 21). After about four hundred years of slavery in Egypt, the Israelites were being delivered. If they left without favor, they would be delivered from labor and pain, from slavery and bondage. But God decided to give them favor, and lo, here they come out with great wealth, new dress, and abundant joy. Wealth generation is a result of God's favor.

Moses lacked Favor

"And Moses said unto the LORD, Wherefore hast thou afflicted thy servant? and wherefore have I not found favor in thy sight, that thou layest the burden of all this people upon me?" (Numbers 11:1). For the most part Moses recognized God's favor upon his life. Favor can be such a shield upon our lives that problems and stress do not flood over us. When Moses, the man of God, saw that stress was starting to take a toll on him, he prayed, seeking the reason for the draining away of God's favor that was strong upon his life. Moses realized that he was productive, efficient, and effective always when God's favor was evident.

The ultimate route map to God's favor is to praise the Lord! Another word denoting the word *favor* in the Bible is the word *loving-kindness.* "Because thy loving-kindness is better than life, my lips shall praise thee" Psalm 63:3).

Because we belong to God through Christ Jesus, we now have received God's favor. God is partial to us because we are His children. He shows us His goodwill and friendly regard. Ephesians 1:3 says, "Blessed be the God and Father of our Lord Jesus Christ, who has blessed us with every spiritual blessing in the heavenly places in Christ."

$

Chapter 24

God Has the Power to Bless

God alone has the power to bless, and His blessings will overtake you. "And all these blessings shall come on thee, and overtake thee, if thou shalt hearken unto the voice of the Lord thy God." Wow! If you meet God's conditions, then His blessings are a sure thing. They will run you down and tackle you. His blessings will seek you out. His blessings will surprise you and seize you.

Since God is the source of blessings, only He can control it, and only He can bestow it. When you open the Bible, the first thing God does in relation to man is bless him. When you dig a little further, you'll find the first Psalm is also about blessings. The first verse of that first Psalm says, "Blessed is the man who does not walk in the counsel of the wicked or stand in the way of sinners or sit in the seat of mockers." Blessed is that man!

Then you go on and follow the lead to the New Testament and the most famous sermon Jesus ever preached—the Sermon on the Mount in Matthew 5. The Lord's most memorable sermon is all about blessings. Blessed are the poor in spirit . . . blessed are those who mourn . . . blessed are those who hunger and thirst after righteousness. It is God's disposition to bless us.

Dr. John Piper puts it this way:

> When God blesses us, it is what he really loves to do. God is not acting in a generous manner in order to cloak some malicious motive. God is not saying inside, "I will have to be generous

> for a while, even though I don't want to be, because what I really want to do is bring judgment on sinners." God is truly acting out his deepest delight when he blesses. His joy, desire, his want and wish and hope, pleasure and gladness and delight is to bless . . . to give the kingdom to his flock.

It is not God's duty or His obligation to bless us. It's something God delights to do out of the greatness of His heart. He blesses you with health and consolation in times of hardship. He blesses you with friends and intellect, with eyesight and hearing. He blesses you with everything from salvation to the satisfying pleasures of good food and great fellowship.

Again God has the power to bless. He possesses this supreme authority for certain reasons, one being "to bless you." You see, God was before all other authorities. Before the world was, God was, and when the world has passed away, God will still stand as the supreme authority.

We must recognize that God's blessings proceed first from His own nature and are part of His revelation of Himself so that we might know His nature, person, and character. It is the nature of God to express Himself. Therefore, He utters Himself forth. God utters forth His sovereign authority through printed words that you and I can read in the Bible. These words are real, dynamic, and created. When God spoke it, it was done. When God said it, His words made it real. When He commanded it, it stood forth. Whatever God said happened. His word will always come to pass. There is power in God's Word. When you believe it, something happens.

When God wants to bless a man, He gives him a promise. Yes, a promise. Go to your Bible and read these promises.

- "I will make of thee a great nation, and I will bless thee" (Genesis 12:2).
- "I will make your name great, and you will be a blessing" (Genesis 12:3).
- "I will surely bless you and make your descendants as numerous as the stars in the sky and as the sand on the seashore. Your descendants will take possession of the cities of their enemies, 18 and through your offspring[a] all nations on earth will be blessed" (Genesis 22:17-18).

- "May God Almighty bless you and give you many children. And may your descendants become a great assembly of nations! May God pass on to you and your descendants the blessings he promised to Abraham. May you own this land where we now are foreigners, for God gave it to Abraham" (Genesis 28:3-4).
- "And ye shall serve the LORD your God, and he shall bless thy bread, and thy water; and I will take sickness away from the midst of thee" (Exodus 23:25).
- "May the LORD bless you and protect you. May the LORD smile on you and be gracious to you" (Numbers 6:24-25).
- "You will be blessed in the city and blessed in the country" (Deuteronomy 28:3).
- "Your basket and your kneading trough will be blessed" (Deuteronomy 28:5).
- "You will be blessed when you come in and blessed when you go out" (Deuteronomy 28:6).
- "The LORD will send a blessing on your barns and on everything you put your hand to. The LORD your God will bless you in the land he is giving you" (Deuteronomy 28:8).
- "The LORD will open the heavens, the storehouse of his bounty, to send rain on your land in season and to bless all the work of your hands" (Deuteronomy 28:12).
- "You will lend to many nations but will borrow from none" (Deuteronomy 28:12).
- "The LORD will make you the head, not the tail" (Deuteronomy 28:13).
- "Blessings are upon the head of the just" (Proverbs 10:6).
- "A faithful man shall abound with blessings" (Proverbs 28:20).
- "For I will give you abundant water to quench your thirst and to moisten your parched fields. And I will pour out my Spirit and my blessings on your children" (Isaiah 44:3).
- "The Lord will open the windows of heaven and pour you out a blessing" (Malachi 3:10).
- "He that is righteous is favored of God" (1 Nephi 17:35).
- "The Lord blesses and prospers those who put their trust in him" (Helaman 12:1).

- “May he give you and your descendants the blessing given to Abraham, so that you may take possession of the land where you now live as an alien, the land God gave to Abraham” (Genesis 28:4).
- “I will bless them and the places surrounding my hill. I will send down showers in season; there will be showers of blessing” (Ezekiel 34:26).

These are the words of God. He has spoken His authority through His Word, and He is speaking forth these blessings in your life. As a recipient of the blessing, you experience a favored life and a rich life with nothing lacking or broken.

When the Israelites were preparing to enter the Promised Land, five times God said to them, “Follow me and you will be blessed” (Deuteronomy 11). Blessing also involves obedience to God.

The Hebrew people were to bless the LORD for the Promised Land that they were to enjoy. They were to thank God and acknowledge His blessings in their lives. Do you bless the Lord for His blessing in your life? How often do you recognize and acknowledge that God has prospered you in school, on your job, in your business, or in the ministry. Remember, prosperity implies that you are doing something. The Bible does not teach that God will drop prosperity out of the sky. Prosperity is applied to what you are doing. In the case of the Hebrew people, prosperity was applied to their livestock, crops, and children. Though prosperity may be the result of God’s blessings, we shouldn’t define God’s blessings by prosperity. Blessing and prosperity are more than money.

As I study Moses’ involvement with Israel, they had experienced redemption from Egypt. Israel had been protected and preserved by God for forty years in their wilderness wanderings, and now they were on the verge of crossing the Jordan River to enter God’s land of promise. If they had learned anything, they had learned that all true blessings flow from God. Man cannot bless!

$

Chapter 25

Be a Blessing

The Lord said to Abram, "I will make you a great nation, and I will bless you, and make your name great, so that you will be a blessing" (Genesis 12:1-4). However, blessings in the Bible come in many forms.

In the first creation story in Genesis 1 God created the great sea creatures, the fish, and the birds and then blessed them all. Later in Genesis Jacob and Esau have a bitter fight over their father's blessing. In the book of Ruth Naomi calls for the Lord to bless Boaz (Ruth 2:20). The psalmist cries, "Blessed are those who walk in the light of the Lord, blessed are those who fear the Lord, and blessed are those who seek God's justice." Blessings are an important part of the biblical narrative.

We don't know much about Abram's life before God's call and blessing in Genesis 12. But we do know Abram's call and blessing from God was a big one, big enough to be remembered for all eternity.

It's that phrase, "you will be a blessing," that stands out to me. Usually we think of blessings only as something given rather than something enacted and embodied. God tells Abram, "Be a blessing." The translators of the Revised English Bible chose a different wording. "I will make your name so great that it will be used in blessings." Literally in the Hebrew the phrase means this: "So be you a blessing." So I think the English "be a blessing" probably makes the most sense.

But before we go off to be blessings to the people, we need to consider why Abram is a blessing. God said to Abram, "I will make of you a great nation, and I will bless you, and make your name great, so that you will be a blessing." Far too often today we switch that order around, claiming

God is blessing us while what's actually happening is that we're neglecting our call to be a blessing to others. God doesn't tell Abram, "Be blessed," but rather He says, "Be a blessing." We have to give blessings in order to get blessings from God. That is intentional blessing and living.

It is always God who is doing the blessing, and only in response to God's blessing can Abram be a blessing to others. God calls, and Abram responds. Abram was blessed. Then he hit the road. Sure, the blessing may have sounded nice at the time, but I'm sure it wasn't comfortable, leaving one's country, kindred, and father's house to move to an unknown land.

Did you notice that the text doesn't tell us Abram's spoken response? It just says, "So Abram went as the Lord told him." Can you imagine what Abram must have said and thought? *What is God thinking? I'm seventy-five years old and have no children. How will my family be blessed? Ain't nobody got time for this.* Nevertheless, Abram obeys the call from God.

When God calls Abram, there are no conditions. He doesn't say, "If you do this, then I'll bless you." God doesn't even say, "I'll bless you now, but you'd better watch it. If you screw up, I'll take it all away." No, the Lord's call and blessing of Abram is unilateral. Unconditional. Unbreakable. It's that same covenant of God's love that we have today.

We need to get our minds into the culture that surrounded Abraham. The blessing that God gave to Abraham was not just some specific gift or a specific promise of possessions. The blessing consisted of the words that God spoke over Abraham's life. So repeat after me out loud, "I am a blessing, and I bless Abraham's children." Now according to that Scripture, you will be blessed. However, even more than our speaking out a blessings upon Abraham, we have the Logos word of God, which says, "And if ye be Christ's, then are ye Abraham's seed, and heirs according to the promise" (Galatians 3:29). Abraham s blessings have been given to us through the very Word of God!

Abraham understood by the blessing of the words that were spoken into his life that he was well favored by the Lord! You should give where you are blessed because when you do, you will receive a blessing. That's the background of the famous statement in Malachi 3:10, "Bring the whole tithe into the storehouse, that there may be food in my house." The temple in Jerusalem contains certain rooms where the grain given by the people (in payment of their tithes) was stored. The priests received an allotment of that grain, which freed them up to minister directly to the people. The poor were also given food from those same storage rooms. When the people of Israel failed to tithe, the priests were not paid and had to begin farming. This meant that the religious life of the nation was hindered and the poor were not cared for. Ironically by failing to tithe, the Israelites were ultimately hurting themselves.

Giving where you are blessed is an enormously important guideline to remember. Are you blessed by your church? Then give there. Are you blessed by a radio or TV ministry? Then give there. Are you blessed by the work of a missionary in a distant land? Then give to help that missionary. Do you see important things being done by an inner-city ministry? Then write a check to help them out. Do you believe that a certain Christian college or Bible institute is doing something worthwhile to train the next generation of Christian leaders? If you do, then let your support be seen in a visible way.

Give where you are blessed, and you will receive a blessing. This is nothing more than what Jesus said in Luke 6:38, "Give, and it will be given to you. A good measure, pressed down, shaken together and running over, will be poured into your lap. For with the measure you use, it will be measured to you." Sometimes I think we read this verse and don't take it as literal truth. When Jesus said, "It will be given to you," He based that promise on the truth of who God is. He is a generous, benevolent God who loves to give good things to His children. Because it is in His nature to give, He will always give more to us than we will give to Him. This to me is the first law of Christian giving: You cannot outgive God.

We give because we have received. God gives to us, and then as we are blessed, we give to others. As a result, we receive a blessing, which causes us to keep on giving. God loves a cheerful giver and rewards those who give because they want to.

It's important to sow favor in order to reap it in your own life. You have to sow in order to reap. The more seed you have sown, the larger your harvest will be. The more you are blessed, the more you can be a blessing. When you sow sparingly, you will reap sparingly (2 Corinthians 9:6-10). And the one way to reap a harvest of God's favor in your life is to sow favor. Make sure that you are helping someone else and showing favor to that person. As it is said, "What you make happen for others, God will make happen for you." Any time you plant a seed—weather it is in finances, friendship, favor, or any other area—that seed leaves your hand, but it doesn't leave your life. It is working in the supernatural realm, bringing you a harvest in that same area.

Don't be deceived. If you sow, you will reap.

$

Chapter 26

Increase

God gave Israel a great land. It was a land flowing with milk and honey. What a wonderful place for God to bring the Israelites after they were slaves in Egypt for 430 years. Let's think about this land flowing with milk and honey.

Milk comes from cows, goats, and sheep. Honey comes from bees. But for cows, sheep, and goats to produce milk, they have to have plenty of fresh green pasture. For bees to give honey, they have to have plenty of flowers, fruits, and vegetables to gather pollen as they pollinate the plants. So a land flowing with milk and honey would be a rich land, a land with plenty of fresh green vegetables, flowers, fruits, and pastures.

How rich was this land the Lord gave to the children of Israel, this "land flowing with milk and honey"? The Bible reads in 2 Chronicles 5:2-6, "Also king Solomon, and all the congregation of Israel that were assembled unto him before the ark, sacrificed sheep and oxen, which could not be told nor numbered for multitude."

When Solomon was dedicating the temple of the Lord, the sacrifice was such that they could not count the oxen and sheep that were sacrificed. So how rich was that land that the Lord describes as "a land flowing with milk and honey"? Richer than anything you and I can even imagine.

The real question we need to think about is this: Why does God give us this wealth? Does He give us this wealth to build large mansions or buy homes and cars? Yes, but He also gives us wealth to be a blessing to others.

Increase simply means divine addition. To increase is to multiply, and it takes multiplication to replenish the earth. Increase agrees with the law of nature. It is evidence of living. Absence of increase shows that death is imminent. It is therefore mandatory for every living thing to increase, or else its existence stands the risk of abuse. God, the Creator, is God of increase, and He mandates every living thing to increase.

The Holy Scripture reported that Jesus increased in wisdom and stature and was in favor with God and man (Luke 2:52). The Bible declares unequivocally that it is enough for the servant to be exactly like his master (Matthew 10:25). Therefore, you are mandated to increase and reject stagnation.

The power of increase is not within the realm of man. It is not in the ability of man to bring increase in his efforts. A man and woman can be joined together to produce a seed, yet the power of increase is not within them. You can draw a plan perfectly, but this could not bring good results because it is not in man to increase, or else there will be no poor man on earth. It is God that gives increase. God is behind your increase. First Corinthians 3:7 says, "So neither the one who plants counts for anything, nor the one who waters, but God who causes the growth."

Until you know that increase is important and that it is God who gives increase through the instrumentality of the Holy Spirit, you never will achieve anything. Jesus told His apostles to remain in Jerusalem until they were endued with power from on high, knowing very well that without this power, they would not achieve anything in their ministry.

Do you trust in God's promise to increase you? Do you trust in God's promise to lead you to greener pastures because you are tired of dead-end places? Ask God to enlarge and increase the place of your tent.

God has a breakthrough for you, and the way to get ready is to enlarge your tent. Begin by enlarging your thinking with a repentance that lines your thoughts up with God's. Start thinking His thoughts, which are revealed in His Word. "Be transformed by the renewing of your mind, that you may prove what is that good and acceptable and perfect will of God" (Romans 12:2). "Eye has not seen, nor ear heard, nor have entered into the heart of man the things which God has prepared for those who love Him. But God has revealed them to us through His Spirit" (1 Corinthians 2:9-10). Jabez enlarged the tent of his heart and prayed to the LORD, "Oh, that You would bless me indeed, and enlarge my territory" (1 Chronicles 4:10), and God answered his prayer. "Lengthen your cords, and strengthen your stakes."

There are walls to demolish, rooms to enlarge. There are paradigms that must to be shifted. Give up your small ambitions. Your life was meant to be so much larger than you have ever known. Start believing, start imagining, and start speaking of the prosperity of God that is coming to overflow into your life. God is able to do "exceedingly abundantly above all that we ask or imagine, according to the power that works in us" (Ephesians 3:20). Dream bigger and expect more, for His power is in all those who trust Him. The power of God for every breakthrough you and I will ever need is already at work in us.

"For you shall expand to the right and to the left." The Hebrew word for *expand* is *pawrats*. It is the word for breakthrough. It means to break out, burst forth, come broadly, spread out, and increase. In the year of the Lord's favor, you will breakthrough to a larger place. Former boundaries no longer apply, for God is bringing increase and abundance. "The LORD give you increase more and more, you and your children" (Psalm 115:14).

"Your descendants will inherit the nations, and make the desolate cities inhabited." This is not just about you and me. It is about our children as well. There is an inheritance at work. "Behold, children are a heritage from the LORD" (Psalm 127:3). "A good man leaves an inheritance to his children's children" (Proverbs 13:22). God has a powerful inheritance in us that will affect all nations. "Ask of Me, and I will give the nations for your inheritance, and the ends of the earth for your possession" (Psalm 2:8). In this inheritance the desolation for the nations will come to an end, for in the year of the Lord's favor they shall become a habitation of His glory.

If you know the Lord Jesus Christ, this is your year to experience the favor of God, to walk in His freedom and wholeness, even to experience His anointing and power to minister that same freedom and wholeness to others. If you have not yet received the Lord Jesus Christ, this is the year of invitation. "Behold, now is the accepted time [the time of favor]; behold now is the day of salvation" (2 Corinthians 6:2).

Now is the time to enlarge your thinking, your imagination, and your heart to the promises of God, for He is breaking you out to enlarge your territory. He who is able to do exceedingly abundantly above all you can ask or imagine will bring His power to bear in your life. In fact, if you know the Lord Jesus Christ, it is already at work in you. Therefore, regardless of the outward circumstances of your present situation, you must give praise to the Lord. Don't hold back. Break loose with loud shouts of joy, for God is bringing His breakthrough into your life. God must also increase His favor upon your life because you are the seed of Abraham! It follows that God's favor brings good things into our lives!

In our lives God gives us promotions and raises and changes to better jobs because we have His advantage through Christ! Do you expect even simple favor like a front row parking space? You should! When you regularly expect the favor of God, you will receive it all the more. You cannot predict when or how the favor will manifest itself. You can only have faith that it will come! Every time you experience a supernatural advantage, even when it is small thing, declare it out loud right then and there! In those times declare, "That was the favor of God!" We will receive more of God's favor when we express thankfulness for His benefits. When we have an attitude of gratitude, we will receive more favor! Shout it out loud, "That was the favor of God on my life! Thank You, Lord!" Regarding favor, God performs more than enough. "Now unto him that is able to do exceeding abundantly above all that we ask or think, according to the power that worketh in us" (Ephesians 3:20). Realize that the same verse says, "According to the power that worketh in us!" We need to be working (i.e., exercising through faith and through our words) the power that God has made available within us! Think about Abraham's blessing as it is expressed in Genesis 12:2, "I will bless you [with abundant increase of favors] and make your name famous and distinguished, and you will be a blessing [dispensing good to others] (AMP).

God's presence increased upon Abraham's life as Abraham found favor with God. All you have to do is study Abraham's life, and you see favor. Genesis 24:1 says, "And Abraham was old, and well stricken in age: and the Lord had blessed Abraham in all things." God had favored him in all things. The favor of God in Abraham's life caused his wife's barren womb to conceive.

$

Chapter 27

Keys to Increase

Prosperity from God's point of view means well-being in every area of life. If you recall the words of Malachi 3:11, it says, "And I will rebuke the devourer for your sakes, so that he will not destroy the fruit of your ground, nor shall the vine fail to bear fruit for you in the fields." At times we forget that we can earn excellent wages, but if things are constantly breaking down or we have many unexpected expenses, that money won't go far. As we bless the Lord with our resources, He will protect and bless what we have so our finances will more than cover our needs.

Let's dissect the word *prosperity* a little further. Prosperity is a close relative of abundance. Abundance indicates that a person possesses an exceptional degree of material or spiritual blessings regardless of whether or not human effort is involved. So abundance comes whether you make any effort for it or not. It is always a gift from God but not necessarily a special gift for human effort. That's abundance.

Prosperity is success that comes to those who have been active in achieving it and/or by divine grace usually as a result of effort. So the difference between abundance and prosperity, generally speaking, is that for prosperity there's effort that has to be made. It's just not given as a freewill offering.

Prosperity is success that comes to those who have been active in achieving it, and Ecclesiastes 4:9 tells us prosperity is the state of those who "have a good reward for their labor." We see that Solomon understood that principle as well. So abundance is a gift from God regardless of effort. Prosperity is a gift from God for effort.

Let's look at some Old Testament Scriptures and examples of prosperity to get a feel for how God expressed it. The Old Testament does present prosperity in a different way than the New Testament, and I think you will find it eye-opening in the way it is handled.

In the Old Testament prosperity is pictured in terms of fruitful work, resulting in sustenance of physical life. Because Israel was an agrarian nation, biblical prosperity was in large part agricultural. King David's prayer in Psalm 144 is a good summary of the Old Testament idea of prosperity. The types of blessings that are generally given in the Old Testament are a result of obedience to the covenant, obedience to God's Word, and living His way of life.

His blessing is dependent on obedience. But does the blessing of prosperity always mean that it is a well-deserved blessing from God? We know that the wicked prosper, so obviously that can't be true. In the Old Testament context of the covenant, prosperity is a sign of God's approval and blessing. Throughout the entire Old Testament we see example after example of how prosperity was given as a direct blessing for obedience.

New Testament prosperity seems to change somewhat from Old Testament prosperity and its implication of righteousness. It is mainly an Old Testament premise that earthly prosperity is an extension of a person's spiritual life. Jesus Christ coming to earth as a flesh and blood human being was in itself a massive reversal of the Old Testament idea of prosperity—just the fact that He came as a human being.

In 2 Corinthians 8 Paul speaks of Christ becoming poor compared to His previous glory and wealth so that we can become spiritually rich as a result of His sacrifice and by following His example. We will prosper—and are prospering—as a result of the sacrifice that Jesus Christ made. Second Corinthians 8:9 reads, "For you know the grace of our Lord Jesus Christ, that, though he was rich, yet for your sakes he became poor, that you through his poverty might be rich."

Prosperity of itself is a blessing from God. How we use it is of the utmost importance. Abraham is a typical example of a wealthy, God-fearing man who used his wealth righteously. He was a very generous man. Do you remember the example of Lot, when they were looking down on the land and Abraham told Lot to choose the best land for himself. So Abraham, although greatly wealthy, had the right attitude and was willing to lose the best of what he had to give to someone else. The right use of wealth requires general liberality toward those in need.

Did you know that the Holy Scripture says more about ministering to the poor than it does about most other important topics? That's because if we truly want to be sold out to God, we will want His compassion toward the truly needy more than anything else.

You see, God designed us in His own image, and His image is one of deep love, concern, and compassion, especially for those who are truly poor and discouraged. He wants us to be so in love with Him that we have His heart, which means that we love those He loves and that we long to minister in the same way He does, to meet the need of the moment. That is one of the main reasons He wants to bless us.

Now that isn't to say that He doesn't just want to bless us to show us His love, but we must keep our wits about us regarding finances and refuse to fall for the deceitfulness of riches, which often leads saints away from God and to spiritual shipwrecks.

Here are a few Scriptures that show God's take on the subject:

- Psalm 107:8-9 says, "O, that men would give thanks to the Lord for His goodness, and for His wonderful works to the children of me! For He satisfies the longing soul, and fills the hungry soul with goodness."
- Psalm 35:27 says, "Let the Lord be magnified, who has pleasure in the prosperity of His servant."
- Deuteronomy 8:18 says, "And you shall remember the Lord your God, for it is He who gives you power to get wealth."
- First Corinthians 4:7 says, "What are you so puffed up about? What do you have that God hasn't given you? And if all you have is from God, why act as though you are so great, and as though you have accomplished something on your own?"
- Second Corinthians 9:11 says, "You will be made rich in every way so that you can be generous on every occasion, and thought us your generosity will result in thanksgiving to God."

Can you see the broad expanse covered by God's definition of prosperity? If not, I ask that you meditate on 2 Chronicles 20:20. It says,

"Believe in the Lord your God, so shall ye be established blessed; believe his prophets, so shall ye prosper."

The Bible tells us in Third John 2, "Beloved above all things it is my wish for you to prosper and be in health even as your soul prospers." By this verse alone we know beyond a shadow of a doubt that it is God's will for us to prosper.

There is an attack on the economy now more than ever. Interest rates are the highest. Fuel, which dictates the price of all kinds of transportation, has been raised countless times this year. Rentals, which get half of most people's income, have gotten more expensive. With the standard of living going up like it has been going, where will your help come from? As a believer, you must know how to operate in the kingdom of God's system. It's time to turn on the spiritual laws that govern prosperity and increase. When you understand and know how to activate these spiritual laws, they will result in prosperity and increase.

Increase comes from God. And God wants to bless you and increase you. It is His will for you to increase in every area of your life. It is His will for you to prosper so that you are not impoverished. Deuteronomy 8:18 confirms that God has given you the power to get wealth. If God didn't want you to be wealthy, He wouldn't have given you the ability to get wealth. So call forth your blessing because only what comes from you will come to you. This is the law of receiving. Jesus was a good receiver. He freely gave, and He freely received. This is also the key to increase.

$

Chapter 28

A Healthy Perspective on Money

Did you know that the Holy Scripture refers to money 2,084 times. That's ten times as many times as it mentions either salvation or faith? That means that the subject of money is important to God. So how should Christians regard money?

Sometimes as adults we find that we've grown up with skewed notions and emotions when it comes to money. For some who grew up with unmet needs or who may at least have had that perception, money has a magical way about it. Little children are known to make wishes, and they believe their wishing can either erase problems or make good things happen if they wish hard enough. Unfortunately some of those beliefs grow with us into adulthood, which is why we often see people gambling away huge sums of money their families need for food and shelter. They believe their luck will change if they only believe hard enough in the magic.

On the other side of the coin, we find a different scenario—those who were raised in an atmosphere where the pursuit of money was the end-all and be-all of life. They may have had plenty, yet somehow it never seemed to be enough. That is the exact definition of the word *want*—a belief system that totally disagrees with the reality of the situation. For those people, everything revolves around securing their future by stocking away as much money as they can in any way they can for as long as they can get away with it. In this category people either perpetrate or are prey to get-rich-quick schemes. If we're wise, we'll realize that any time something seems too good to be true, it usually is, and it will end in catastrophe for those who fall prey to such trickery.

Any way we look at it, it's easy to be superstitious about money, and the Devil loves that. I find it particularly interesting that he tries to tempt us by using exactly what we think we want. That's why we need to get our hearts right with God so that we are completely secure in our place in God and can distinguish His voice from the voice of the Devil and can also shed superstitions about money (or the lack of it).

If we are to walk in the glory, we must first settle the issue of finances. How is it that we as believers are to get our needs met? Scripture tells us that we aren't to worry as the world does.

Matthew 6:24-34 puts it this way:

> No one can serve two masters, for either he will hate the one and love the other or he will hold to one and despise the other.
>
> You cannot serve God and mammon. For this reason I say to you, do not be anxious for your life, as to what you eat, or what you shall drink; nor for your body, as to what you shall put on.
>
> Is not life more than food, and the body more than clothing? Look at the birds of the air, that they do not sow, neither do they reap, nor gather into barns, and yet your heavenly Father feeds them.
>
> Are you not worth much more than they? And which of you by being anxious can add a single cubit to his life's span? And why are you anxious about clothing?
>
> Observe how the lilies of the field grow, they do not toil nor do they spin, yet I say to you that even Solomon in all his glory did not clothe himself like one of these.
>
> But if God so arrays the grass of the field, which is alive today and tomorrow is thrown into the furnace, will He not much more do so for you, O men of little faith?
>
> Do not be anxious then, saying, "What shall we eat? Or 'What shall we drink? Or 'With what shall we clothe ourselves?"
>
> For all these things the Gentiles eagerly seek; for your heavenly Father knows that you need all these things.
>
> But seek ye first the kingdom and His righteousness, and all these things shall be added to you.
>
> Therefore do not be anxious for tomorrow, for tomorrow will care for itself. Each day has enough trouble of its own.

Notice the phrase "You cannot serve God and mammon." If you're like me, you probably assumed that the word *mammon* referred to money. But that isn't true. It's actually the name of a Canaanite idol Israel worshipped during that time. Apparently this idol's (spirit's) job was to convince them that there would never be enough. While they worshipped him, they then became a slave to money and its pursuit, hoping to fill the perceived void. In contrast, we as believers are to give our hearts to God, to sit at His feet in order to get wisdom and direction, and then *rest in Him* and use the money He gives us to bless His kingdom, generous toward others in response to God's great love and the security we feel in our restored identities.

In other words, we are to see money in a whole different light than unbelievers. We are to seek first the kingdom of God, and then He will bless us with El shalom (His spirit of peace and well-being with nothing missing and nothing broken) and the tools (including money) that will be His hands extended. If we truly believe the resurrection restored the blessing and everything stolen at the fall, we can walk in completeness and power as mighty warriors. From that place we can be confident that God has already anticipated our needs and will meet them with extra to share.

$

Chapter 29

A New Take on the Upcoming Wealth Transfer

Proverbs 13:22 tells us, "A good man leaves an inheritance for his children's children, and the wealth of the sinner is stored up for the righteous."

Many believers get quite excited, especially over the second half of this verse, believing that it refers to them. But there are qualifications they may not be aware of. The truth is that we must balance that truth with the Scriptures in Psalm 37:21 and Proverbs 22:7.

Psalm 37:21 says, "The wicked borrow and do not repay, but the righteous give generously." And Proverbs 22:7 says, "The rich rule over the poor, and the borrower is servant to the lender."

According to current popular belief, people think they can borrow as much as they want and at the year of jubilee:

1. All debts will be erased.
2. All slaves will go free.

But they forget the third part of the teaching on the year of jubilee.

3. Land and possessions revert back to their original owner, which, in the case of today's borrowers, is *the bank*.

That's why the Holy Scripture says to owe no man anything and to be a lender rather than a borrower because we become enslaved to the one we owe.

With that truth in mind, we must rethink the idea that we get to keep what we have paid for with borrowed money that we have not repaid because, according to God's Word, the bank will actually repossess those things.

Just look at what's happening today and tell me it's not so. Repossessions of houses, cars, land, and valuables are at an all-time high, which only confirms the truth. If we read on to Proverbs 22:8, we see, "He that sows wickedness reaps trouble; and the rod of his fury shall be destroyed." Here we see that the Lord calls borrowing money to spend on our lusts as "sowing wickedness" that does not please God. And if it's true that God sees these people as wicked, who then are the righteous? Those who (as Psalm 37:21 says) "give generously" and owe no one anything. In the end, the wealth of the wicked will be transferred to those who are not in debt.

No doubt you've read about what happened during the Stock Market Crash of 1929. After World War I money flowed like water, and people who thought the gravy train would never end financed everything they owned with bank loans. When the value of things suddenly plummeted, just about anything—even very expensive things—could be purchased for pennies on the dollar. That is what economic analysts predict will happen again, and when it does, those who have even a little cash on hand will be able to buy what they need for little or no money. The banks will make losers of everyone who owes.

This may be an entirely new concept to many people, especially in our easy-payment economy. But a person doesn't have to be a genius to see the logic in this argument. He just has to pay attention to what's happening around him to see that this is so. Having said that, let me also strongly suggest that you do all you can to pay off your debts, including your mortgage.

"Pay off my mortgage? How is that possible?" you may ask. Well, it may take a little adjustment in your thinking, but let me ask you this question: Do we or do we not serve a God who owns the cattle on a thousand hills? Can He not make the impossible possible for His beloved if we seek to obey His commands? Now is the time to end the purchase of frivolous things and seek to become debt-free. In the end, the wealth of the wicked will go to those who are righteous in God's estimation—those who are debt-free.

$

Chapter 30

A Promise is a Promise

What I truly love about God is that He answers to no one about the decision-making process. There is no committee, no board to approve His decisions. He doesn't take a vote or look for a consensus. He is sovereign, a completely self-sufficient ruler with no counselors, no governing boards, no confidantes, no senate or congress, no electoral colleges, and no debate. He just makes an executive decision, with love reigning supreme, to bless us.

Whatever God thinks He says. Whatever He says comes into being with a simple command. Whatever He has in mind always comes to pass, whether or not people like, understand, or believe it.

I am writing this today because God ordained it that I would be here on this day at this time in this place, writing down these things. If God hadn't ordained it, it wouldn't have come to pass. Knowing this, I spend very little time worrying about the opinions of others. In the end, nothing people say can derail the marvelous plans God has in mind for us—that is, unless we allow it to undermine our faith.

Some of us spend far too much time asking others what they think when in reality their opinions don't matter. It makes no difference what any of us thinks about these things. In the end, only God's opinion matters. And if that's so, consider what the Holy Scripture says about us:

- If God's Word says we're blessed, then we're indeed blessed!
- If God's Word says we're healed, then we can take that to the bank!
- If God's Word says we're successful, then we are successful!

- If God's Word says we're anointed, then we are anointed!
- If God's Word says we're blessed with finances, then we're wealthy!

The thing we need to keep in mind is this: Our prayers are actually answered the instant we pray, as supported by the Scripture passage in Daniel 10:12-13, "Then he said unto me, 'Fear not, Daniel; for from the first day that thou didst set thine heart to understand and to chasten thyself before thy God, thy words were heard, and I am come for thy words. But the prince of the kingdom of Persia withstood me one and twenty days, but lo, Michael, one of the chief princes, came to help me.'" That means that we can be confident that God has answered our prayers, even if we don't see instant manifestations. We just need to pray against the hindrances stopping them and thank and praise God as if they're already ours.

In the beginning God's plan to bless man was thwarted for a time because Adam sinned, but Jesus came, died, and rose from the grave, taking the keys of death, hell, and the grave along with eternal punishment for sin. And as we mentioned earlier, He also restored to us all the covenant blessings that God gave Adam in the garden. And not only that, He restored the El shalom blessing, meaning that at the resurrection He restored everything we need for life and godliness with nothing missing and nothing broken. Indeed, our entire well-being and confidence was restored when Jesus rose from the grave! That's the incredible truth, and I'll keep on repeating it because it's key to our success, whether men want to believe it or not. Liars can't stop it. The Enemy can't block it. Those who hate you can't cancel it. It's a done deal!

In reality, the only thing that stops it is our unbelief. And right now we're casting down doubt and unbelief so we can grab hold of these remarkable truths—truths that will change our lives if we let them.

Henry Ford once said this: "Whether you think you can or you can't, you're right." In other words, we will only go as far as we believe we can, so we limit God when we refuse to believe He can do all things and even use us to change the world. How are you limiting God?

Our God, who is rich in mercy, declared that He would bless the house of Israel, people of faith, His children, those with whom He made and kept the covenant. So regardless of the state of the union and the chaos and upheaval in governments and economies, God's truths never change. He loves us, and He is going to bless us!

Social security can go bankrupt. The dollar can fail. Gas can go over $10.00 per gallon, but we can still expect to be blessed.

Remember the Old Testament story of Jacob? In Genesis 29-30 we see how his Uncle Laban cheated him out of his betrothed cousin, Rachel, even after Jacob worked seven years in exchange for her hand in marriage. At that point Jacob could've become bitter and unforgiving, but instead he chose to let go of anger, giving it to God and believing that God would vindicate him.

When Jacob finally decided to leave, his father-in-law begged him to stay and tend his flocks because God had also blessed him because of Jacob. After some discussion Jacob agreed to stay if his father-in-law paid him with the least favorable of the livestock, those with speckles, stripes, and spots, so that they were easily distinguishable from the flocks of his father-in-law. In the end, the ones with stripes and spots had multiplied beyond all expectations and were far more robust and fertile. When all was said and done, Jacob departed from there a rich man simply because he had a heart after God.

Deuteronomy 28 goes into great detail about blessings and curses.

> Now it shall be, if you will diligently obey the Lord your God, being careful to do all His commandments which I command you today, the Lord your God will set you high above all the nations of the earth.
>
> And all these blessings shall come upon you and overtake you, if you will obey the Lord your God.
>
> Blessed shall you be in the city, and blessed shall you be in the country. Blessed shall be the offspring of your body and the produce of your ground and the offspring of your beasts, the increase of your herd and the young of your flock. Blessed shall be your basket and your kneading bowl. Blessed shall you be when you come in, and blessed shall you be when you go out.
>
> The Lord will cause your enemies who rise up against you to be defeated before you; they shall come out against you one way and shall flee before you seven ways.
>
> The Lord will command the blessing upon you in your barns and in all that you put your hand to, and He will bless you in the land which the Lord your God gives you.

> The Lord will establish you as a holy people to Himself as He swore to you, if you will keep the commandments of the Lord your God and walk in His ways.
>
> So all the peoples of the earth shall see that you are called by the name of the Lord; and they shall be afraid of you.
>
> And the Lord will make you abound in prosperity, in the offspring of your body and the offspring of your beast and the produce of your ground, in the land which the Lord swore to your fathers to give you.
>
> The Lord will open for you His good storehouse, the heavens, to give rain to your land in its season and to bless all the work of your hand; and you shall lend to many nations, but you shall not borrow.
>
> And the Lord will make you the head and not the tail, and you only shall be above, and you shall not be underneath, if you will listen to the commandments of the Lord your God, which I charge you today, to observe them carefully.
>
> And do not turn aside from any of the words which I command you today, to the right or to the left, to go after other gods to serve them.

In this passage He is talking to those who belong to Him, who minister in true worship to the Lord and offer up sacrifices to Him with the right heart attitude. In other words, God is saying He will bless His children as we serve Him, supplying the finances, the people, and the power we need. He is saying that the blessing will be so huge that it will continually overflow down to our children and grandchildren. It will be far more than just enough because of the character of the incredible God we serve, the one who truly delights in blessing His children.

In Numbers 6:24 we see a blessing sometimes known as Aaron's benediction. It's quite familiar to most of us because we've heard pastors use it in the pulpit. "The Lord bless you and keep you. The Lord make His face to shine upon you and be gracious to you. The Lord lift His countenance upon you and give you peace."

However, in the original Hebrew it is actually translated this way: "The Lord will bless you, and keep you. The Lord will make His face to shine upon you and be gracious to you. The Lord will lift up His countenance upon you, and give you peace."

Looking at it that way, we can see that it lines up with the blessings in Deuteronomy 28, with no ifs, ands, or buts about it. And because these are promises made by a God, who cannot deny Himself or go back on His Word, we can rest, knowing He is trustworthy to do what He promised.

$

Chapter 31

Why the Gospel of Provision is so Vital Today

Many of us grew up during an era when churches simply preached that God loved us enough to send Christ, while it was somehow understood that we were on our own when it came to making it in the real world. But that kind of gospel doesn't hold water anymore. It's incomplete and sounds ridiculous to someone in need.

I'm here to tell you that our gospel had better be about God's provision. And here's why: Unlike in third world countries, in America we've been blessed to the place where most of us could usually provide for ourselves, whether God was involved or not. The average American—even some who have quite low incomes—still had a roof over their heads and food on the table. Many wage earners held the same jobs for thirty years, with reliable incomes they could count on. But in recent years things have drastically changed, and many faithful, hardworking people have lost their jobs and their homes and can no longer provide the barest necessities for their precious families.

At that point, this phrase takes on new meaning: "When a belly is hungry, the gospel is all about food." When the desperate father of a homeless family is forced to live with them in the family car, trying to keep his children warm and fed, you can bet the gospel becomes all about provision. In that instant, this dear man isn't worried about the "sweet by-and-by." He needs to hear that our God loves him and his family and wants to provide for them. No longer can we simply preach the gospel without ministering to the needs of desperate people. Our gospel should be all about provision because showing love any other way falls far short of the real thing. We need to be Jesus with skin on, ministering to the needs of the moment.

To take it one step further, let me also add that the poverty mentality may sound pious and holy, but it bears little resemblance to the plan God envisioned at creation. God's ideal world for Adam and Eve was lush with provision of every kind. Nothing was lacking, broken, or missing. He delighted in His children and wanted them to be blessed in every way, displaying to the world God's great love and glory. Let no one try to convince you otherwise.

We are to be enthusiastic givers, lining up with heaven in everything we do. We are not to look at circumstances and the way things appear to our physical eyes, but remember that heaven's resources are unlimited. We are to guard our ears and refuse to listen to bad news, which only produces fear (2 Timothy 1:7). It's also essential that we guard our tongues (Proverbs 18:21) because "death and life are in the power of the tongue, and they that love it shall eat the fruit thereof."

It's easy to find ourselves saying, "I've never had anything of value. My parents were poor, and so were their parents before them." Those words actually become our destiny as we repeat them. But it doesn't have to be that way. Jeremiah 17:7-8 and Psalm 1 agree on one thing—that those who love the Lord will be blessed. "He shall be like a tree, planted by the waters, which spreads out its roots by the river, and will not be anxious in the year of drought, nor will cease from yielding fruit."

Psalm 24:27 tells us, "Let them shout for joy and be glad, who favor my righteous cause and let them say continually, 'Let the Lord be magnified, who has pleasure in the prosperity of His servant.'" God does not take pleasure in our poverty or hunger. He takes pleasure in prospering us.

This is why our words are so important. We will only have what we can believe and speak in faith.

Once He gave Adam and Eve dominion over the earth, God actually stepped back, promising to be there for them. Since that time He has limited Himself to working through people to whom He has also given dominion and the power to bind and free with our words. When something happens, it will happen because of us, or it won't happen at all. God had a perfect plan and designed each of us with passion and a purpose. Destiny allows us to discover the reason we are here, and once we occupy that place, operating through the Holy Spirit, provision and prosperity are a natural result. When we start operating in that destiny, God will bless us.

The stark truth is that it takes money to live, money to do the work of God on earth, money to finance ministries that preach the Word, money to travel into all of the world in order to preach the gospel, even if it's by way of radio, television, or the Internet. It requires massive amounts of money to evangelize every corner of the earth, providing Bibles in every language. And believe me when I say that according to Matthew 24:14, every corner of the world must hear the gospel in order to usher in the return of Christ. So in essence, we are delaying His return if we fail to do our part to finance and give prayer support to that evangelistic effort.

The question we must then address is this: How can we help others when we can't even help ourselves? How can we reach out and pay someone else's heating bill when we can't even cover our own expenses? It's impossible! Believe it or not, our God isn't at all surprised to know these things.

These are times when our preaching must line up with real life. Our preaching should be so relevant that people can grab ahold of it with great passion and excitement. If God truly has a plan for a future and a hope for each and every individual alive today, that means that He also has a plan to provide for them. Real love is the most relevant message ever preached.

The reason that for years the church failed to preach provision is that it got into acting the part of the Holy Spirit, failing to trust that blessed people would use their blessing for kingdom purposes. But it's not our job to be the Holy Spirit. Whether we believe it or not, the Holy Spirit doesn't require our input because He can manage just fine without us. The whole unvarnished truth is that we need to get in line with His plan in order to walk in the spirit and love with the kind of love Jesus showed.

What does that mean? What did Jesus do when He walked from city to city, preaching the gospel? He met people along the road who were in desperate need, and He met the need of the moment so that people could actually hear His message of salvation.

If pain or hunger distracts you from the message of the gospel, what good is the gospel? It needs to meet the need of the moment. And when we lay hands on people and pray for their healing or an end to their hungry or when we love on those who feel lost and abandoned, we *are* the gospel. We are Jesus with skin on.

$

Chapter 32

Good News

Are you ready for good news? I am here to tell you that God is about to send increase into your life—increase in finances, increase for your children, increase for your church, increase on the job, increase in your home, and increase in your business. It doesn't matter who planted or who watered the seed. It's the Lord who brings the increase.

In conclusion, the favor of God is on us once we've lined up with the scriptural principles. Because He is mindful of us, our past has been blessed, but our future will be far greater than our past. Get ready for the promise. Get ready for provision—a blessing just for you. It's coming big this year. It will be huge. Get ready for the following:

- A God-ordered outpouring
- A God-sent blessing
- A twofold harvest (just for you)

Your time has come. It's time to declare *FBI*, favor, blessings, and increase, over your problem; *FBI* over your issue and your sickness; *FBI* over your trouble: *FBI* over your ministry; *FBI* over your children; *FBI* over your money; *FBI* over your health; *FBI* over your church; *FBI* over your job; *FBI* over your atmosphere; *FBI* over your neighborhood; *FBI* over your spouse; *FBI* over your mind; *FBI* over your life; *FBI* at school; and *FBI* in your marriage.

I decree and declare the following over you today in the mighty name of Jesus:

- Your life is not cursed.
- Your life is not ruined.
- Your life is not over.
- Your life is blessed.
- You're blessed in the city.
- You're blessed in the field.
- You're blessed when you come and blessed when you go.

Over everyone reading these words, I speak prophetically and say the following:

- The blessing of the Lord be upon you.
- Never again will you be without.
- You shall live in houses that you did not build.
- You shall inherit land you did not purchase.
- You will reap where you did not sow.
- Your territory shall be enlarged.
- Your ministry will flow in abundance.
- Your life will be enriched.
- You will have everything you need.

Get ready for favor. Get ready for blessings! Get ready for increase—more than you can hold in your hands and more than you can handle. Reach up and grab it. Here it comes.

- Personal blessing
- Territorial blessing
- National blessing
- Universal blessing
- Miraculous blessings
- Payback blessing
- Showers of blessing
- Abundant blessings
- More than enough blessings
- Bonus blessings
- Dimensional blessings

- Supernatural blessings
- Divine increase
- Promotions
- Increased assets
- Blessings overflowing

It's time to open your mouth and announce to the Enemy that you're walking in favor, blessing, and increase. Be blessed!

$

About the Author

Bible teacher Barbara Bryant is a published author as well as a mentor and popular speaker of the gospel. Her previous books include Compensated Suffering, Gifted Inspiration, and Stedmon Makes Me Laugh. Her passion is encouraging others to find their destiny in Christ. Her outreach ministry includes books, teaching tapes, and DVDs, all designed to help people attain God's best for their lives. Barbara makes her home in Southern California. Visit her website at www.barbarabryant.com.